Mindfulness Plain & Simple

Mindfulness Plain & Simple

A Practical Guide to Inner Peace

Oli Doyle

This edition first published in Great Britain in 2014 by
Orion
an imprint of the Orion Publishing Group Ltd
Orion House, 5 Upper St Martin's Lane,
London WC2H 9EA
An Hachette UK Company

5 7 9 10 8 6 4

A CIP catalogue record for this book is available
from the British Library.
Paperback ISBN: 978 1 4091 5676 5

Designed in Kingfisher by Geoff Green Book Design, Cambridge

Printed in Great Britain by
CPI Group (UK) Ltd, Croydon, CR04YY

www.orionbooks.co.uk

*For seekers of truth
and lovers of happiness*

Thank you

Without my amazing wife Ren, this book would be a pale shadow of what it is. Thank you always. Likewise our two crazy kids, Liam and Freya, continuously remind me that the here and now is where I should be.

Thanks to my parents James and Tricia, my brother Phil and my sister Abby for your support and for sharing this experience called life.

My work is inspired by a few people who won't even realise it. I would like to thank Carolyn, Llevellyse, Janet, Jen, Ellen and Julia, your stories keep reminding me of why I do this.

Thanks also to Brooke, Ali, Kathleen, Paula, Ann and Janine, you are the best team I could ever work with.

I would like to thank my spiritual teachers, some of you I have met, others I have not. Everlasting thanks go to Ekai Korematsu Osho, Eckhart Tolle, Byron Katie,

Osho and Adyashanti. I bow at the feet of Bodhidharma, Mahakashyapa, Gautama Buddha and all who contributed to the meditation traditions of the world. Your gift is truly lasting.

Thank you to Jane Graham Maw for being my guide through this process. And finally, thanks to Jillian Young and the team at Orion for seeing something they wanted to be a part of. I hope that together we can share this work far and wide.

Contents

Introduction   xi

Part One: The Great Conspiracy

1   What Is Wrong with Us?: The real cause
of suffering   3

2   The Stories of Our Lives: Thinking, beliefs
and happiness   21

3   The World of Thoughts: I think, therefore
I am (unhappy)   33

4   Emotions: Making friends with feelings   47

Part Two: The Mindful Way

5   Life without Stories   61

6   The Essence of Mindfulness   75

7   Unconditional Happiness   85

8   Peace Every Moment   101

Part Three: Walking The Path

9   Smoothing the Path: Overcoming obstacles in
     your practice   117
10   Questions and Answers   127

Finally...   133
Resources   135

Introduction

As long as you live lost in thought, you are not really living – you are a ghost. A life experienced only through the mind and its stories is like a black and white picture of a beautiful sunset: drab and dreary. If you are sick of this dreary life, stuck in pain and suffering, wondering where to go, what to do ... congratulations, your journey has just begun. Mindfulness practice can free you from this painful, confusing life. But what is mindfulness, and where did this practice begin?

Two thousand six hundred years ago, the Buddha discovered something that had been right under his nose all along: freedom from the mind. The Buddha is not mentioned much in the coming pages, but his discovery and the practices that arose from it are the basis of this book, i.e. mindfulness. The question Buddha asked, and the topic of this book, is 'How can I free myself from the pain of this world?' The answer is simple: *Be here now*. Putting this into practice, however, is difficult because of our conditioning and because we are so accustomed to listening to the thoughts that pass through our minds every day. This book is an exploration of the human mind, detailing its current state of dysfunction and describing the path to health and happiness.

Part One explains in simple detail why it is that humans are so very unhappy in the first place. It will take you on a journey through the dysfunction and confusion that lead to such suffering on this planet every day, discussing the fundamental problems in our dealings with thoughts and feelings that create that unhappiness in the first place.

Part Two details the path of mindfulness in everyday life, describing what life in the present moment is like, and how you can begin this journey today.

As you travel on this journey, you will find simple mindfulness exercises that are designed to give you a taste of mindfulness practice, a foundation from which to start. They are not a definitive list, as mindfulness can be practised anywhere, any time, regardless of what you are doing, but you may find it helpful to have some written guidelines as a starting point. Written exercises can never replicate the power of working with an experienced teacher, but they can give you a taste that may inspire you to continue. There are also ten free audio classes that accompany this book. These classes are designed to deepen your mindfulness practice and are available for you to download at www.mindfulnessplainandsimple.com.

It is also worth noting that, although the exercises are segmented, divided into specific activities, they also overlap. For example, mindfulness of breath, walking and listening can all be done at the same time, although you might find it easier to focus on one aspect at a time in the beginning.

As you move through the chapters, I suggest pausing to try each exercise, at least for a few minutes, then looking for opportunities in your daily life to practise that aspect of mindfulness. Return to reading when the time feels right, but be sure to make space to put these skills into action. Through applying what you learn, you will find that mindfulness slowly but surely becomes a part of your everyday life.

When you practise mindfulness, there are some important principles and practicalities to keep in mind, and I would like to outline these before we begin. Understanding the points below will help make your adventures in the present moment all the more enjoyable.

Formal and Informal Practice

Formal practice means the deliberate practice you set time aside for in your day, like sitting mindfully for ten minutes in the morning. Informal practice means being mindful at work, with friends, or anywhere else in your normal, day-to-day life. They are really the same thing, but for the purposes of explanation, it helps to create a distinction between the two.

Formal practice is the platform for bringing mindfulness into your life because it allows you the time and space to deepen your practice, while continuing to practise informally in your everyday life can strengthen your awareness as you stay connected to the moment in more challenging situations. In this way, formal and informal practice continually support each other.

If you sincerely want to be mindful in daily life, then regular formal practice is very helpful. This is why going to a regular class or meditation session is beneficial, as it gives you the support and encouragement to continue practising. Alternatively, CDs, DVDs, podcasts or other online resources can provide an opportunity to practise with incredible teachers without leaving home. But, regardless of which resources you use, the most important thing is that you keep practising every single day. And the tips below will make daily practice a whole lot smoother.

Consider Your Timeframe

- Before you start, decide how long you plan to spend on your formal practice. Consider starting with a shorter amount of time (ten to twenty minutes) and building up to a longer period of time if you wish.

- Formal practice should support your life, not overtake it, so beware the urge to meditate instead of taking care of your life. All those daily activities are an important part of life and of mindfulness practice, so watch that you aren't neglecting anything.

- Each period of mindfulness practice is as it is, and forty minutes is not necessarily better than ten. What matters is that during that time you are focused and aware – as much as you can be.

- Consider setting an alarm to mark the end of the session. This allows you to focus on the practice instead of checking your watch. This is especially helpful if your time is limited due to other commitments, like getting ready for work.

Remove Distractions

- Remove as many distractions as possible. Turn off or unplug your phone, make sure televisions and radios are switched off, and make sure no newspapers or reading materials are visible.

- Try to practise at a quiet time of day in your house.

- If someone wishes to practise with you, make sure you are both clear on what you are doing to avoid distracting each other.

- Talk to your housemates or partner about what you are doing and ask for their support in not distracting you during your formal practice.

Awareness vs Concentration

- Awareness is not a skill, it is something that grows organically over time given the right conditions. Every time you notice a daydream, you are returning to this state and helping it to grow within you.

- Awareness is open, it takes in everything, whereas concentration implies sustained focus on a particular thing. Awareness is like listening to a song, while concentration is like listening intently to the words without paying much attention to the whole composition.

- We practise awareness by allowing everything to be as it is, including our thoughts and feelings. We let everything come into our open awareness, and we notice when we have become fixated on a particular thought.

No Right, No Wrong

In the workshops I run, people often seem worried about practising mindfulness 'right', but there is no right or wrong as long as you continually return your focus to the present each time your attention drifts away. The suggestions about how to practise and what to pay attention to are there to support your practice, they are not commandments, although your mind may try to turn them into rules that you must follow in order to be 'good at it'. All you need to do when this happens is to notice what your mind is doing and return your attention to your body, your breath and your mind. Continually doing this is mindfulness; there is nothing else to it. Get lost, come back, get lost, come back – this is peace and joy.

As you read the following pages, take notice of the old patterns of dysfunction in your own mind, see the stories that keep you lost in thoughts of the past and the future, and spend time practising the exercises, which are the heart of this guide.

Finally, before we start, congratulations! You are undertaking the most rewarding and amazing journey there is, the journey into yourself. It is challenging, and you will get lost at times, but just keep going, just practise. Freedom is waiting, and finding it is easier and simpler than you ever imagined.

PART ONE
The Great Conspiracy

Hello, and welcome to an exploration of the great conspiracy, the greatest myths and fabrications ever created by the human race. Over the coming chapters, we will explore and debunk the most popular myths about what causes the pain and suffering experienced by humans everywhere, every day. Freedom from pain can only start when that pain is seen as unnecessary, and when an alternative, peaceful and harmonious way of life comes into view. When this new way of life is experienced and understood, the old, apparently normal, way of life can be seen as a life of unnecessary suffering and confusion. You may already see this, and maybe that is why you are reading this book in the first place. Alternatively, this book may strike you with seemingly new insights, but in fact they are things that you already know. So, welcome to freedom from pain; welcome to the beginning of a mindful life.

CHAPTER ONE

What Is Wrong with Us?:
The *real* cause of suffering

The human world is filled with pain, confusion and suffering on an individual and collective level to the point where it almost seems normal, even inevitable. Humans become more miserable as a species every year, while the self-help shelves proliferate with books promising the answer, the miracle cure, like the snake oil sellers of old.

In the West, we have more psychologists, counsellors, social workers and mental health professionals than ever before, but the number of people suffering from depression, anxiety and other mental illnesses continues to rise. In the midst of all this, more and more people are seeking a way out of pain and suffering as it becomes more unbearable. However, as you may have already discovered, changing your diet, your job, your partner, your appearance, or some other external thing, does not bring peace. And efforts at changing your thinking, improving your self-esteem, or altering your patterns of behaviour still leave you feeling empty, wanting more change, needing ever more improvement.

So, what's going on here? What is it about humans that makes happiness seem so difficult to attain? The rest of nature co-exists in balance and harmony, why are we so different? The answer, in short, is this: humans listen to, believe and follow the instructions of their thoughts. We are lost in our thoughts, they consume our attention most of the time, and they are made up of scary stories about what will happen in the future, or pain and guilt about what happened in the past.

Listening to and believing these stories is the source of our pain, whatever your mind may say. The rest of this chapter will explore what this means and look more deeply at the problems it causes. As we do this, see if you can spot these patterns in yourself as well as in others. *Seeing* the confusing mess your mind creates is the first step towards *untangling* the confusion.

The Human Condition

The majority of humans live in a state of emotional discomfort most of the time. This can range from mild, insignificant worry to more extreme suffering that can lead to nervous breakdown or even suicide. Most of us sit on the milder end of the spectrum with problems perhaps involving body image or self-esteem, never quite feeling secure or good enough. We swarm around in ceaseless activity, searching for the one thing that will make us feel whole and complete, desperate to avoid the negative, self-deprecating thoughts and painful feelings hidden within. Boredom, sadness, guilt and anxiety are seen as an inevitable part of life, to be managed with medication or covered up with distractions and entertainment, but why do we experience these feelings in the first place?

We walk around smiling, terrified that other people (who are actually doing the same thing themselves) will find out that we haven't actually got it all together. This is why someone can commit suicide without those around them having any idea that they were anything other than perfectly happy: their mind told them that no one would understand, that everyone would think they were crazy, that this was the only way out. Thoughts compel people to hide their pain as they drive them to self-harm, a behaviour that is uniquely human. People only hurt themselves because the pain seems inescapable and inflicting physical pain provides temporary emotional relief. Mindfulness can provide lasting relief from this same pain, with no negative side effects.

The way we relate to others is also marked by problems and pain. A 'normal' human relationship is a battleground filled with competition, conflict and suffering. This is not always true, but more than half of all marriages end in divorce, and relationships where some conflict or disagreement is not a regular occurrence are very rare. The same goes for families and workplaces, where conflict of some sort is often seen as the norm. Indeed, the most common perpetrators of violence are members of the victim's close family, meaning that, as a species, we attack those closest to us. This is bizarre behaviour, which would be unthinkable in the animal world – with the exception of minor disputes that establish social position. Why do we physically, emotionally or psychologically attack those we claim to love?

The way we relate to the natural world is equally hard to comprehend. Why do humans seem to insist on destroying the environment we live in? We exploit natural resources far beyond what we need to survive. Millions of us starve while millions more eat just for comfort, damaging their health through excessive consumption. We poison our bodies with all sorts of toxic substances in a desperate attempt to escape the 'inevitable' pain, the pain that seems borne of the frustrations of life, and this is the great conspiracy:

It is not what happens to us that causes our suffering. Our suffering is caused by believing the stories our minds tell us about what happens to us.

Let me explain in a different way. Believing painful thoughts causes pain, even when our lives are wonderful and nothing that happens can prevent us from being peaceful and happy. Only listening to the voice in our heads can bring pain, and that is the human condition.

We listen to, believe and identify with every thought that goes through our minds, and this leads to frustration, anxiety, worry, fear and suffering as we give all of our attention to these stories of the painful past and the frightening future, neither of which has any tangible reality except as a thought in our heads. Even when you are lying in a warm, safe, comfortable bed on a mild summer's evening, you can be sweating from fear and anxiety, from thinking about 'what might happen'. The fear is totally in your mind, which means the antidote is also within you.

Let's look at this in more detail.

The Fearful Future

Fear of the future is seen as a normal and natural part of being human, but if we pay close attention, we can see some scary, painful thoughts at the root of that fear. Without these stories, there is no fear, but if you believe those stories, you will scare yourself stiff! Fear, which includes tension, nervousness, anxiety and worry, is seen as normal and even helpful by many people, who believe that without it we would lack motivation, becoming listless and lazy.

This is partly true: fear motivates many people to do many things, it is the driver behind much of our activity. Some of us continue to go to work out of fear of losing our job, we buy our partners gifts, scared they may leave us and, as a species, our fear of losing economic wealth drives the continuing push for growth at all costs. I believe that much domestic violence is driven by fear, as people who use violence try to maintain control of their partners and children because they are terrified of losing them.

This example shows the destructive effect of action that is motivated by fear, but because our fear of negative consequences motivates so much action, it seems logical to the mind that this fear is needed and useful. This is based on the assumption that without fear, we would not be motivated to do things, which is not the case in my experience. What if your best, dearest friend invites you over for dinner? You know they will completely understand if you can't come, so there is no fear. Will you go, or will you lie at home on the couch? No fear is needed for motivation here, but fear might drive you to go to that boring, dry work dinner instead of seeing your friend, worried about what the boss would say if you weren't there.

In my experience working with mental health issues, in particular anxiety, it appears that fear is what keeps people from doing things they want to do. Fear of negative consequences keeps people in the house, keeps them in the same job, keeps them from talking to new people and making new friends. Fear of the future is a limiting factor, not a driver for growth and activity, and it is also absolutely unnecessary. Without this fear, you can pursue activities not to avoid unpleasant consequences but to enjoy yourself, which fundamentally changes the character of your life. This change is the focus of mindfulness and it will be explained and demonstrated as this book continues, but for now, let's look at another example of the Fearful Future...

Imagine that today is Friday, and that on Monday you are starting a new job that you really want to go well. It would be considered 'normal' not to sleep much and to spend time feeling worried and nervous over the weekend, but what causes all these feelings and this loss of sleep? The mind projecting into the future, imagining what may happen on Monday causes these feelings.

While you are lying awake at 3 a.m., your mind may spend time playing mental movies entitled 'What Will Happen on Monday', movies that unfortunately bear no relation to what will actually happen when Monday morning arrives, although they feel very realistic in the middle of the night. Your mind may also torture you with painful and fearful thoughts about the future such as, 'I'm not sure I can do this job', 'it's way out of my league', and 'it's only a matter of time until they find out I'm no good'. If you look closely, you will see that all these stories cause you pain and that the fear you experience has nothing to do with the new job itself, but is caused by the mind projecting into the future.

So much time is spent thinking about what will happen tomorrow that we barely experience today. The mind then uses the vague memory of yesterday (which we were barely aware of) to predict what will happen tomorrow. Does that sound like a reliable system to you? This constant projection leaves us only vaguely experiencing life, lost in the mind instead, which also means we are lost in the past and the future. I recently started a new job in a field I have not worked in before. Because I was aware of my mind's stories when they arose, I did not experience any fear, nerves or worry in the days leading up to this new start. On my first day I tried to stay mindful, anchored in the present moment, and I thoroughly enjoyed what would have been a nerve-wracking experience for me a few years ago. Let me emphasise that I am no enlightened master, just an ordinary person.

Before we move on, I want to clarify something. When I talk about the 'Fearful Future', I am not talking about valuable, practical activities, like planning your day, your week or your year. What I am talking about is the mental activity that can accompany future planning: worrying, obsessing and dwelling on possible problems. So perhaps it is worth separating future planning into two categories: the *Fearful Future* and the *Fearless Future*.

To summarise, the difference between these two approaches is this: in the *Fearless Future* we live in the now, work with actual information and enjoy the process of planning. In the *Fearful Future* we live lost in mental images, dreading what might go wrong or anxiously anticipating things going 'right'. We work

In the Fearless Future:

- We can plan for practical matters, make appointments and organise our lives.

- We make plans calmly and factually based on the information we have.

- Once these plans are made, we return our attention to the present moment, adapting our plans if new information comes to hand.

In the Fearful Future:

- We spend time thinking about bad things that could happen in the future.

- We go through these events mentally, experiencing anxiety and fear as if they were actually happening.

- We project current 'problems' into the future, for example, if I had no money in my bank account today, I might picture myself as a destitute old man while experiencing fear and anxiety.

with speculative projections of possibility and we lose the ability to enjoy what life is presenting now because we are lost in thought. Hopefully this illustrates that living in the moment does not prevent us from planning and being organised, but it does prevent us from getting lost in painful, scary stories about things that may or may not happen. The next time your mind starts projecting into the future, see if you can become aware of what is happening and notice what emotions accompany these projections.

Let's now look at the mind's other favourite pastime (no pun intended): reliving the past.

The Painful Past

After events take place in our lives, the mind analyses them and, for most of us, starts comparing 'what happened' with 'what should have happened', leading to feelings of guilt, remorse, anger and sadness. The gap between what we want and reality could be called 'The Abyss', and the bigger it is, the more unsatisfactory life seems to be. Most people try to close that abyss by changing their life to fit their preferences, but life refuses to conform to our wishes, leaving us feeling frustrated and unfairly treated. In this book, we will look at the alternative, which is to close this abyss by working with our thoughts, with our story of 'what happened' and 'what should have happened'.

The story of 'what happened' could also be called 'what they did' or 'what I did' and could be compared to 'what they should have done' and 'what I should have done'. The content of the stories doesn't matter as much as recognising the process at work, observing the mental habit of comparing reality – what is – with our imagined ideal – what should be. When we listen to the

The Practical Past vs the Painful Past

People often assume that living in the moment without being lost in stories of the past will inhibit our ability to learn from past experiences and plan for the future, but this is simply not the case. Many species learn from past experiences while experiencing each moment as it is, but humans allow the mind's stories of the past to contaminate our entire lives without necessarily learning much at all. People carry around pain, suffering, grudges and fear, sometimes from things that happened decades before. There is nothing wrong with learning from the past, but the mind can continually replay painful memories accompanied by anger and thoughts that create suffering long after the event. This process not only causes immense pain, it also prevents us from living our lives now; and remember, this is the only life we have.

Constantly replaying these old memories, and dwelling on the thoughts associated with them, leads to similar events occurring in our lives again and again until we are finally able to let go of these stories of the past and move on. This process of reliving the past is more like self-torture than a learning process because we replay all the major mistakes we remember making and relive things that people have done to us. This is what makes up the mind's view of the past, which it then uses as a template for projecting what will happen in the future, which seems understandably scary. When we learn how to live life now, we can learn from the past in a way that is clear and peaceful, and then let it go. This robs the past of its power and makes life infinitely more enjoyable in the process. Freedom from this cycle is available here and now by focusing our attention on the present moment. Take a few breaths and pay close attention to the different sensations you experience. Don't analyse or think about this process, just feel it physically. By using the breath to bring our focus onto this moment, we can start to experience freedom from the mind.

mind's stories about what should have happened, about what others or we should have done, we are no longer experiencing our actual lives, we are instead lost in the mind's tales of the past. This leads to repetition of the same patterns of behaviour, to stress, anxiety, guilt, and to a general apathy toward life in general. Through practising mindfulness, we can learn how to come back to our experience right now instead of staying lost in this perpetual cycle.

Endless Comparisons

Comparing is another mental habit that is a feature of human existence, and this happens continually. It can be clearly seen in the media where systems, movies, ideas and celebrities (among other things) are rated and compared. In our own minds, we can see this through the comparison of ourselves to others as the mind searches for security through superiority. Our minds will think we are 'better than' certain people, which will affect the way we treat them. In turn, thinking we are 'worse than' other people may lead us to be nicer to them, to hide our own opinions until we know theirs and to do things we would rather not in order to gain their approval.

This process also extends to our impression of our lives, with the mind comparing 'my life' to 'their life', as in 'I don't know why he's so miserable, I'd be happy if I had his lifestyle', or, 'I've had it pretty tough, but it's not as bad as what she went through.' This leads us to envy those who appear better off than ourselves and to feel guilty when others are going through something we have been spared, like poverty or war for example. This guilt and envy may seem necessary to inspire us to make changes, but more often they lead to inaction and apathy. When we are engaged in the present moment, we can act clearly and decisively to effect change, if change is needed, without the guilt, stress and anger that arise from these comparisons.

The mind also looks at different parts of our lives and compares them, longing for the good old days and hoping that everything will work out in the future. Stories like 'I hate being old, I wish I were young again. Life was much more fun back then' or 'Life was so much better before I had kids. I can't wait till they leave home so I can be free again' arise in the minds of many people, leading to dissatisfaction with life as it is now. Ironically, after the kids leave home, parents often feel lonely and wish the kids came back to visit more often! Therefore, the mind can never be happy because it focuses on what is lacking in the situation: not enough freedom, too much free time, and so on and so forth.

However, the mind's favourite comparison, and the one that causes the most pain, is to compare 'what is' with 'what should be'. This process involves forming a mental idea of the way things should be – or should have been – then comparing it with the way things are. This is such a normal mental process that for most people it happens totally subconsciously.

For example, you may think your parents should be more accepting, or that your partner should be nicer to you. This can lead to much time spent feeling resentful and upset, due to the unquestioned belief that something in your life *should* be different. Attempts are often made to control, manipulate or impress other people because we believe we need something from them in order to find happiness.

The process of endless comparison eventually causes

a feeling of separation from others who we compete with in order to feel better about ourselves. It also leaves us unable to enjoy the differences between people and situations, to enjoy things for what they are. When we compare and analyse, our experience of life becomes very narrow with no room for anything that exists outside of 'what I want'. We divide life into tiny bits, unable to enjoy the whole picture. Without these comparisons, life is just as it is, no more and no less, and there is no need to change anything – including ourselves – in order to be happy.

The strange part is that none of these processes really give you anything, apart from a huge headache of course. We can learn from the past and plan for the future without engaging in these painful, scary comparisons, which merely prevent us from enjoying life as it is now. Living mindfully is much simpler once you know how, and Part Two of this book will show you how you can start to practise engaging with the present moment instead of constantly looking back and forward.

When does your life take place? Where do you experience everything? Your life takes place now, and you experience everything here. Even thinking about the past or the future happens in this moment, so does the past or the future really exist? I am not suggesting that past events did not actually happen, or that our memories of them are not real, but where are they now? They are stored in the mind as thoughts, nothing more.

However, humans devote most of their attention to these ghosts residing in their minds. No wonder we have problems.

As we continue on our journey through the insanity of our species, we will examine the way thoughts and feelings run our lives in more detail. But first, I invite you to take a few minutes to sit quietly and enjoy our first mindfulness exercise, which uses simple breath awareness to bring peace and clarity into this very moment.

Notice Every Breath

Breathing continues from birth to death and is always with us. Mindful breathing is the basis of every mindfulness exercise in this section, and it is something you can do at any time. Setting aside some time each day to do the following exercise is a wonderful way to experience mindfulness.

1 For a few breaths, use the muscles of your abdomen and chest to empty all the air out of your lungs, then allow them to fill naturally. As you do this, notice what it feels like to breathe in this way.

2 After these few breaths, allow your breathing to find its own rhythm. Let your breathing be as shallow or as deep as it is while noticing:

   • the rise and fall of your shoulders

   • the expansion and contraction of your abdomen

   • the sensation of the air entering and exiting through your nose or mouth

3 Continue to notice how it feels to breathe. Also, pay attention to the pauses between in and out breaths. Notice the silence created by the gap between breaths.

4 Do this for as long as you wish.

Key Points:

- Sit in a comfortable position with your spine straight throughout the exercise.

- Be aware of your breath without getting lost in the mind's judgements. As much as possible, allow thoughts to come and go without getting lost in them.

Remember: Getting lost in thought is part of the process, so when you do, bring your attention back, check that your spine is straight, and return your attention to the breath.

CHAPTER TWO

The Stories of Our Lives:
Thinking, beliefs and
happiness

Thousands of stories are generated every day in every person's mind. As we walk through the world, our minds interpret, project and try to understand *why* things happen. We believe that everything happens for a reason. We also believe that by knowing the reason, we will have more control over our circumstances, but that's another story altogether. We then spend time analysing the situation to figure out the nature of the problem, what needs to change, and how this change should happen. This process can work very well on some levels. For example, if the washing machine is broken, and we can figure out what is wrong, *why* it isn't working, then fixing it becomes an easier task. There is no problem until the next level of storytelling engages, and stories of negativity and 'victimhood' start to arise. Using the washing machine as an example, you could also start asking yourself: *'Why did this happen to me? What did I do to deserve such misfortune?'* This may lead to an argument with reality along the lines of, *'It's not fair. This shouldn't have happened. They should make better washing machines. My husband/wife/partner should have picked a better model.'* Our minds might then start running mental movies with us cast as the victim. We then rise up, berating the white goods store for not honouring the extended warranty, threatening legal action and so on. The result of this storytelling is that we expend a lot of energy without actually doing anything to improve the overall situation. We spend lots of time in our heads instead of living our lives, and these stories start to become our personal 'reality'.

Victims of Circumstance

When this 'poor me' story repeats in our minds, and we believe it to be true, we start to see ourselves as victims of life and unfairly treated by the world. When we wanted one thing to happen, but something else happened instead, we think we have been treated unfairly. When we believe this story of victimhood, we throw mental tantrums (sometimes physical ones too) in a desperate attempt to shape the world into what we want it to be. We believe everyone and everything should behave according to the laws of our minds, but instead they behave according to the laws of nature – the laws of cause and effect. People die when we want them to live. Politicians go to war when we think they shouldn't. Our partners don't spend enough time with us, or they chew too loudly. Our bodies get sick and don't look the way we want them to. The mind constantly creates these stories and because we believe them, we feel stress. Our stress is never caused by the situation, but by believing the stories the mind tells about that situation. Without these stories, there is only this moment, and it is always fine as it is. Believing the stories creates the pain, which we then attribute to the situation.

Shifting Goalposts

Everything in life is as it is, and believing stress-inducing stories about it does not increase our ability to respond to the challenges life brings; in fact, it reduces our overall effectiveness. Believing those stories often leaves us feeling helpless and without hope, unable to do anything to improve our lives. It also makes life seem like a struggle in which we never quite get to our desired destination. This happens because the mind's goals constantly change, and as soon as one thing is achieved, another desire, another goal becomes the mind's main focus. The mind cannot really live in the present moment because the mind is made up of thoughts, and these thoughts are always a trace of the past. Therefore, once a goal is achieved, the mind cannot enjoy the achievement, it can only continue looking at the past and projecting into the future, looking for a new goal to chase. The relief felt at achieving something actually results from the mind being quiet for a moment, and this brings a natural sense of contentment and joy. We then mistakenly associate this contentment with the achievement of goals, when it is in fact your natural state once the mind falls quiet. Instead of chasing endless goals, why not learn how to enter that state any time, anywhere, learn how to live in that state? This doesn't mean we should have no goals, or that we should sit quietly in a cave for the rest of our lives. It simply means that, whatever we are working towards, the present moment becomes our main focus instead of the end result. This means that, regardless of success or failure, we can enjoy our lives, taking pleasure in each moment as it comes. This brings quality to our actions and increases our success in all endeavours, as well as making us people who spread peace and joy wherever we go. All this is available this instant by simply returning to this moment, to our life.

In later chapters, we will explore the positive, strong and proactive qualities of acceptance, but for now, let's return to the story of 'Me'.

Me and My Story

As we go through life believing all of these little stories about daily events, the mind begins to create a self-image, which is essentially a thought, or a bundle of thoughts, about who we are. If this story were made into a movie, it could be called:

'What I Think Everyone Else Thinks About Me'.
Coming soon to a theatre near you.
Written, directed and produced by Me. Starring Me.

This self-image begins to take shape in childhood, when we believe that every event in our lives is caused by us. When things happen that we interpret as good, like success, good feelings or people being nice to us, we may start to develop a *positive* self-image. Self-help books and counselling often concentrate on creating, improving and maintaining this self-image, as does much of our mental activity. Like political spin doctors, we are mostly concerned with how we appear to the outside world, so that people think well of us, and we can finally believe the 'I am a good person, I am good enough' story. We try to convince others that we are good, and we bargain: 'I'll say nice things about you – to your face anyway – if you do the same for me', we argue, we justify and, finally, we feel tired, incomplete, insecure and like we are not good enough. We get totally caught up in our thoughts and completely lost in the story.

Believing the story of your life stops you from fully experiencing life as it really is.

Life is mysterious and doesn't conform to the linear, logical ways of the mind, or, more accurately, the mind is unable to understand the ways of the world while it is obsessed with developing, enhancing and maintaining a positive self-image. What happens is exactly what happens, we cannot escape from or change it, but we spend a lot more time arguing with reality than responding to it. Consider how much time and energy we waste listening to the mind chatter on and on about what is wrong with our lives, what needs to change so we can be happy, and what we and others are doing wrong. Now ask yourself: Does all this complaining, worrying and arguing actually achieve anything? The mind has a thousand good reasons why things *should* be different, but they *aren't!* Things remain exactly as they are; they don't change, despite the mind's protests. I am not suggesting that things don't change over time. What I am saying is that no amount of complaining can change your experience *right now*. If there is something you can do to improve a situation, by all means do it. If there is nothing you can do right now, at this moment, then leave it alone. This isn't just common sense, it is the path to peace, learning to be peaceful in situations the mind doesn't like. When you can allow this instant to be exactly as it is, when you are peaceful *inside*, no external situation can make you suffer. But instead human beings insist on fighting with the outside world, which guarantees frustration, struggle and suffering. People extend this argument with reality to include themselves; believing thoughts like: 'I'm too fat/skinny/poor/ugly/stupid', and so on. The only reason we feel the need to improve our self-esteem is because we are listening to these thoughts. Without them, the ideas we have about our faults and problems evaporate.

Going Beyond Self-Esteem

You may ask, however, 'What's the alternative, and what's wrong with having good self-esteem?' To answer the second part first, there is nothing wrong with having a positive self-image, but as you may have noticed, maintaining a positive self-image means staving off the negative voices, rationalising supposed failures and working to repair our egos when we come off second best. All of this is a tremendous waste of energy when the alternative, living in the present as a mindful, aware human being, couldn't be more straightforward. Of course, 'straightforward' does not always mean 'easy'. The mind is a complex organism, and we have been practising listening to it for most of our lives. Trying something radically different is going to be a challenge, not because it is complicated or difficult, but because the mind attracts our attention again and again. However, if we continue to practise mindfulness, our ability to connect to the present moment will become stronger, and our lives will become more peaceful. The core of mindfulness practice is learning to observe our minds, becoming aware of our mental patterns, of our thoughts and feelings. When we start to *observe* these phenomena, we can stop getting *lost* in them, take a step back from the mental chatter and shift our awareness to the present moment. When our attention is anchored in this moment, problems and stress disappear and are replaced by peace and contentment. As our practice continues over time, this peace becomes our normal state as more and more attention is devoted to *now*.

The Power of Mindfulness

In my work with people suffering from mental health issues, I have often been astounded by the change that comes over people after doing just five minutes of mindfulness practice. I have seen people who are so caught up in their story that they are speaking rapidly, shaking and crying, become calm and peaceful to the point where their original 'problem' loses all importance. From this point on, these people have been able to calmly assess their options and decide on their best course of action. If this sort of relief and peace is available to someone experiencing very challenging circumstances, imagine what is possible for those who make mindfulness a part of their day-to-day life. The joy and contentment available to everyone is beyond comprehension, and discovering it is as simple as learning to observe your mind.

So, here is the good news. If you feel like your life is missing something, if you feel incomplete, useless, not good enough, or if life seems like a big mess that is too big to clean up, you can be free of that 'life' without having to clean it up bit by bit. I remember once thinking about all the past events I needed to come to terms with in order to be happy, and it just seemed endless, overwhelming and absolutely impossible. However, I discovered that I was able to let go of most of the stories my mind was telling me about those events through practising mindfulness. This is true freedom from a past that only still exists in our minds. When we become more aware, more focused on the present moment, the past loses its power, and the future no longer scares us because the stories of the mind are seen as just that: stories. We then see these stories as no more than vague opinions that cannot be substantiated, not words of wisdom that must be followed. Freedom from stories is peaceful and joyful, and the following exercise will give you a glimpse of that peace right now, so read on as we continue our journey through the mind.

Notice Every Thought

Learning to pay attention to thoughts without getting lost in them is at the heart of mindfulness practice, and it is something that can be done at any time without interfering with your daily activities. When you try the exercise, treat your thoughts like cars driving past the front of your house: you can see and hear them, but there is no need to chase them, you can simply allow them to come and go.

1 Sit down and quietly take some mindful breaths. Be intensely aware of the physical sensations of breathing.

2 As you do this, watch for any thoughts being produced by the mind. Be as alert as you can, watching the thoughts and waiting for the next one to appear.

3 Allow each thought to come and go in its own time. There is no need to try to get rid of or change those thoughts, just observe them.

4 Continue for as long as you wish.

Key Points:

• You need not sit down in a quiet spot to practise this exercise; you can do it anywhere, any time.

- Mindfulness of thought is about allowing thoughts to be as they are, so just observe them without getting lost or getting into a struggle with those thoughts.

- Do not concern yourself with the content of the thoughts, but with the process of observing them coming and going.

- Try to continue this practice throughout your day by noticing each thought that arises. When you find yourself lost in thought, bring your attention back to your experience in the present moment.

CHAPTER THREE

The World of Thoughts: I think, therefore I am (unhappy)

The way we relate to our thoughts drives our human obsession with the past and the future, and these thoughts consume most of our attention most of the time. This leads to a multitude of problems, which we will explore in this chapter. As you read on, notice any insights that arise, as well as noticing the mind's commentary about what you are reading. This 'noticing' is the start of freedom from thoughts, so let's begin by working out what we are dealing with.

What Is a Thought?

This question can provide a great deal of insight into the power (or lack of power) that our thoughts have over us. So, what is a thought? A thought can seem powerful, knowledgeable and important, and as human beings we often listen to every thought that passes through our minds. But, in reality, a thought is no more than an opinion, usually about some aspect of life. The mind observes the world and generates opinions (thoughts) to try and make sense of what is happening and to understand why it is happening. For example, if your partner is angry, the mind might generate thoughts to try and figure out why this is happening and how it relates to you. This could include thoughts like: 'Is he (or she) angry at me? What have I done? What am I doing with this person? They should lighten up, I don't like being around angry people...' and so on. The mind generates a running commentary about life, and if not much is happening, the mind fills the empty space with memories, future projections, song lyrics... whatever it takes to fill a silence the mind finds intolerable.

Thoughts are really no problem, but life becomes problematic when you start to believe these thoughts. Take, for example, an angry partner. Believing the thought that 'they should lighten up' leads you to a feeling of resentment, and you end up getting angry with them for being angry. You might then withdraw into yourself, or conversely, attack your partner verbally, and before long, you are not speaking (although you can't remember why) and the whole mess (which started because they were angry at their boss) takes two days to sort out. During those two days, you feel angry, sad, disappointed and rejected, all because you are believing the seductive, convincing voice in your head, the master storyteller. This voice, apart from generating pain and stress, will tell you that your partner is causing your pain. But without the painful stories, would you still be upset? Incidentally, your partner got angry in the first place because they believed their thoughts about their boss. Indeed, believing thoughts is the source of conflict all over the world because it is impossible to attack someone without believing some thought about them, about why they deserve it, about why this is the only way.

But My Beliefs Support Me, Don't They?

The short answer is no. A belief is no more than a thought that we believe, and a thought is no more than a story. There is no need to tell ourselves stories – even nice ones – about the world in order to be peaceful and happy. The reason we like our nice beliefs – the nice thoughts that we believe – is that they to some extent counteract the nasty stories the mind produces and they give us hope of happiness in the future. However, most of these stories are two-sided anyway. Take, for example, a belief that many people would say supports them: the belief that after we die, we go to heaven or are reincarnated. Buried within this belief is the possibility that we will go to hell or be reincarnated in some hellish realm, or disappear altogether. The mind can then use this threat as leverage to control our behaviour, turning life into a guilty exercise where we try to balance out our past transgressions in order to reach a future salvation. This is exactly what we saw the mind doing in the previous chapter, i.e. worrying about the past and projecting into the future.

There are two paths in life: listening to the mind, with its endless stream of judgements, beliefs and thoughts, or living life in this moment.

Spending time listening to, cultivating and protecting those beliefs takes our attention away from the present moment. It is also exhausting because if something happens that suggests our belief is wrong, the mind feels threatened and feels the need to spend time using logic, justification and validation to stabilise the belief, or it must come up with something new if the belief is no longer sustainable. Just notice what happens when someone contradicts or undermines one of our strong beliefs. We attack their argument, their credibility and their credentials in order to safeguard the beliefs we identify with. This is exactly what politicians do in election campaigns. Why does a different opinion generate so much anxiety and anger? Because it threatens a belief that we see as a part of 'Me', it threatens 'my belief'. If the other person is right, it means I am wrong, worse than them, not good enough. If we are not aware of this process, we can easily get pulled into arguing and fighting over something relatively trivial. Something that supports happiness and peace will not create war like this, it will allow others to be as they are.

Continuous Thinking

Another characteristic of thoughts is that they don't seem to stop, at least for most of us. Thoughts come one after another until we are exhausted and we need to sleep. Then, when we wake up, the running commentary picks up right where it left off. This is why we can't seem to 'get away from it all' when we go away on holiday because we are actually taking 'it' with us! People have said to me, 'I just need a holiday from my mind', and this is precisely why drugs and alcohol are so popular. For many, a night of peace and quiet inside their head is well worth the side effects; indeed, many have died trying to escape the mind's running commentary through these means. So, get drunk, take drugs, get a lobotomy or learn to live with it, OK? This is society's unspoken view, hence the popularity of approaches that try to sweeten up the mind through positive thinking, building self-esteem and trying to avoid situations that trigger painful thoughts.

The mind tells us all these horrible stories, like 'You're a horrible person and everyone knows it', and we believe them, leading us to feel bad about ourselves. The mind then says, 'There must be something wrong with you, feeling sad all the time. Everyone else is smiling, so they must be all right. Better get yourself off to the self-help section and learn about positive thinking!' The mind loves all these self-improvement regimes because they provide a goal to work towards, creating the illusion of a perfect future. These regimes also give the mind something to criticise you about later on: 'See, you can't even do positive thinking properly, you useless waste of space!' I believe that these approaches will become less popular once people realise that rather than trying to make the mind tell nice stories, we can just stop believing those stories in the first place and stop listening to the mind so intently. When we learn how to be mindful, we can have peace, we can be free of these painful stories, without all the effort and activity required to try and manipulate the mind into telling nicer stories.

Ceaseless, Senseless Activity

Human life is characterised by non-stop activity from birth to death. The only time most of us sit still is to eat or watch TV. I believe this is why TV is so popular; it gives us a break from the mind and an excuse to sit and do nothing. At other times, we are on the go all day, performing a multitude of tasks to stay occupied. Check for yourself and notice whether you ever *totally* stop, or if your mind keeps going every waking moment.

I live in Melbourne, Australia, and it isn't uncommon to see someone on the train listening to music while reading a book at the same time. I once saw someone doing both things while walking, and I thought their mind must be very noisy. Have you ever wondered what all those phones, car radios and TVs do for us? Why we are so addicted to these distractions? The reason is that they drown out the mind. I have worked with people diagnosed with schizophrenia who do exactly the same, listening to loud music to drown out the voices. And it seems that everyone else is doing this as well, although they would not be considered mentally ill. Interestingly, there are new and successful treatments for people who hear internal voices that involve learning to notice the voices without getting lost in them, as we do with our thoughts in mindfulness practice. If you have seen the movie *A Beautiful Mind*, you may remember that John Nash did exactly this in order to manage his delusions, and we can all learn to manage our own delusions in the same way. By 'delusions', I mean the endless stories created by the mind, which we don't need to get lost in. Instead, we can watch them come and go, we can learn to observe them instead of believing them, a practice that leads to peace and joy.

Distractions and entertainment are popular largely because they provide relief from the mind's commentary. People who compulsively eat basically do the same thing: they listen to their mind and give in to its orders. The mind then lets up for a few seconds before proceeding to berate the person for binge eating. Whatever our distraction of choice, it gives us a moment's peace, or at least it seems to. However, over time, the more we give in to the mind, the worse the compulsive behaviour becomes and the more chaotic and painful life becomes as we torture ourselves with memories of all the things we 'should not have done'. The mind then seemingly becomes even more powerful.

Peace cannot be found through obeying the mind, or through trying to placate it. True peace comes when you learn to observe the mind instead of complying with it, but we will come to that later. Distractions appear necessary because the mind seems powerful; it won't be quiet and, unless we block it out, there is no rest. The mind is actually power*less* if we don't listen to it and don't follow its commands. Ask your mind this: 'If I don't obey you, what are you going to do?' The mind can't do anything but produce more thoughts, which is why it uses logic and justification to make its desired course of action seem to make sense. It is a voice of complaint, like a letter to the editor: 'Dear sir, you are useless and nobody likes you. This is proved by...' and so on. Taking life advice from the letters page of a newspaper would be pretty unreliable, and listening to your mind isn't much different. In fact, those letters are ghostwritten by the mind, with people doing the mechanics of the writing and signing their names to them. The whole human world is just an external representation of the human mind...

The Mind Externalised

Why do you think the world (and possibly your life) is so complicated? It is because the world is the mind externalised. What I mean is that when people live identifying with a noisy mind, believing that these thoughts are 'me', they create a noisy world. Their lives and the society they live in reflect their state of mind. This is clear when we look at friends who are extremely negative, and nothing seems to work out for them, while people with a more positive state of mind seem to experience much more success. However, you need not be 'positive' in order to succeed because there is no greater success than having freedom from thoughts, which makes so-called success or failure relatively unimportant. This brings more and more peace and joy into our lives day by day, while listening to our thoughts makes our lives and our societies more logical, rational, rigid and complicated.

When I have travelled to less 'developed' countries, I have noticed that life seems simpler, less complicated, and often the people seem happier than they do in the West. I believe this is because people in those countries are less identified with their minds, leading to societies that are more laid back and stress-free. In Guatemala, if you want to get the bus somewhere, you stand by the side of the road and the bus stops. You get on, tell the conductor where you are going, and they tell you how much to pay. They then take your money and give you change. In big cities, if you don't stand exactly at the bus stop, the bus just keeps going. If you get on a tram without the correct change, you can't buy a ticket. If you don't have a ticket, you get a fine. The mind creates rigid systems of rules with defined penalties if we step outside the rules because it basically distrusts human nature and believes that if left to our own devices, humans would descend into anarchy. In less mind-identified societies, there are fewer rules, and time in general is less important.

Our own lives are also reflections of our minds, so people who constantly fight, argue and complain are putting their inner state on display. Peaceful and happy people are more at peace with their minds, more connected to the present moment and, therefore, more mindful. A busy mind makes a busy life, whereas a quiet mind creates a quiet life. It isn't all that complicated really, it is just a simple matter of cause and effect. So, if your life seems chaotic and busy, check the state of your mind. If you can't seem to find peace, look inside. Peace is not something that starts from the outside and filters in; it begins with our inner state and then radiates outward. That is why angry protests against wars are such a waste of time and energy. Fighting for peace? Let's be serious. How could fighting and being angry ever create peace? They are totally incompatible. World peace begins when we learn to deal with anger effectively instead of striking out at others. It begins with us, with peace inside which is felt by the people around us.

World peace is not merely the absence of war, but the deeper, collective peace that arises when people stop believing their thoughts, and that is what this book is all about.

Thoughts vs Reality

Believing our thoughts causes pain because the thoughts often clash with reality – with life as it really is. The thought could be as simple as 'I wish I didn't have to work today', or it could be thoughts about why that person shouldn't have left you. Whatever the clash is, *any time you believe a thought that says life should be different from what it is right now, you will suffer.* It is that simple. Believe a thought that says, 'Life should be different; something is missing', and you will hurt. Don't believe it, and you won't. Byron Katie, in one of her many wonderful books, calls this 'The thought that kicks you out of heaven,'[1] and it is the mind's attempt to control the world in order to protect itself. But who can control the world? Many dictators and conquerors have tried and failed. There are countless examples, both historical and current, of such people causing misery and suffering to themselves and others, all in the service of a set of beliefs. Perhaps if these dictators had learnt mindfulness, they could have stayed at home and left the rest of the world alone. Either way, I am sure they

1   Mitchell, Byron Kathleen, *I Need Your Love – Is That True?,* Random House, 2005, p.9.

would have been happier and enjoyed their lives more. We can't even control our own bodies, which get sick and die without our consent, so how can we expect to control the external world? It is insanity even to try, and it is also totally unnecessary because what happens will always happen whether you like it, hate it or pretend to like it but secretly hate it.

Direct Experience

As we start to practise mindfulness, we learn to pay attention to our experiences instead of the mind's opinions about our experiences. This is very liberating. Who knew that vacuuming, doing the dishes or cleaning the toilet could be so much fun? My mind certainly never told me that! Paying attention to what happens instead of mentally arguing with it is the beginning of that holiday from our minds. Actually, you may find that your mind isn't so bothersome anymore, like that annoying cousin that finally grew up. Inner silence becomes a part of life, and things seem to run more smoothy without all those mental tantrums caused by life not giving us what we wanted. This freedom will be explored more in the next section, but for now, let's continue our exploration of the human mind with another mindfulness exercise.

Find the Gaps

This is an exercise in noticing space and silence, an important part of mindfulness practice. If you are aware of silence, you are not lost in the mind because it is impossible to 'think about' silence. Why? Because thought is mental noise, so as soon as it arises, the silence is obscured. Try this straightforward exercise and see what you notice.

1 Sit in a comfortable position with your spine straight.

2 Breathe mindfully for a few breaths. Notice the pause between breaths, however slight it may be. Be aware of that gap between breathing in and out.

3 Pay close attention to your thoughts. Watch them intently without judging their content. If judgements arise, simply notice them and continue to let them come and go in their own time.

4 Look for gaps between your thoughts, spaces in which the mind becomes silent. Be alert and aware of these gaps and notice the internal silence.

Key Points:

- There may be no apparent gaps, depending on how busy your mind is at the time. If there seems to be no gap, just keep watching your thoughts without getting lost.

- When you notice a gap, allow it to be as long or as short as it is. It is easy to become attached to this silence and to prefer it to the noise of the mind. This attachment is itself a thought, so notice the mind's story that silence is better than noise and allow that story to come and go like any other.

- Try this activity for a few days, do it as often as you can, and see what happens. You may be surprised to find silence even in noisy places, or that the noisy mind can make even peaceful circumstances seem chaotic.

Freedom from the mind is as simple as watching it without getting lost, so try it. Find the gaps in between thoughts and bring more and more awareness to the patterns of the mind each day.

CHAPTER FOUR

Emotions: Making friends with feelings

M̲ost of us play a game with our emotions, and the game reminds me of one I played in primary school. I don't remember the name of it, but everyone had a sling tucked into their waistband, and we would run around the basketball court trying to take other people's slings without losing our own. If you lost your sling, you were out of the game, and the last kid standing was the winner. This may seem a strange analogy, but most of us chase pleasurable emotional experiences while trying desperately to avoid any so-called 'negative' emotions, and this leads to a situation similar to the game, with people running around like crazy, looking over their shoulders in a flurry of movement as they chase 'good' experiences, desperately trying to avoid 'bad' ones.

The emotions we experience as humans living in a society obsessed with 'feeling good' are now so pathologised that we can get Valium because we feel mild anxiety. This is no solution whatsoever; in fact, I believe it intensifies the cycle because people become hypersensitive to their feelings, learning to medicate them away. This symptom-based approach does not solve the root problem, which is the relationship you have with your thoughts and feelings.

As life continues, for most of us the habit of running from the emotions we dislike and chasing those we like is strengthened by practice and by observing those around us. We remain unaware that these emotions are triggered by listening to that pesky running commentary provided by our minds. We may even be unaware of why we feel the need to indulge in certain behaviour. Compulsive behaviour, or an addiction, is anything that you feel unable to stop doing, even when you know that the costs outweigh the benefits. So, what gets people back to the bar, to the casino, to the drug dealer or the refrigerator? Painful thoughts drive us to do all these things, and by understanding the way our thoughts and feelings interact, we can start to see through these conditioned patterns. To better explain this process, let's look at a step-by-step version of events.

1 The mind produces negative thoughts, e.g. 'You really need to lose some weight.'

2 We believe this thought, which leads to feelings of anxiety and worthlessness.

3 The mind suggests eating some of that cake in the fridge in order to make us feel better.

4 Feeling overwhelmed by emotion, we give in and eat two pieces of cake.

5 The mind then abuses us for eating cake, calling us 'fat and lazy'.

6 We return to step 2, and the cycle continues.

Looking at this process in this way, we can see its circular nature. It may seem to start with a feeling, but behind that feeling, we find thoughts saying negative things about us or the situation we are in. The feeling in this type of scenario can often be a sense of boredom, which is in fact an expression of the mind's dislike for the present moment. The thoughts that lead you to eat the cake will normally be much more subtle and persuasive than the above example, with the mind saying things like, 'Go on, just one bit of cake won't hurt. A little bit every now and then is OK. Besides, you've been pretty good this week, you deserve a little treat.' Normally, everything the mind says makes sense, and it appeals to the part of us that wants the cake, but, once we have eaten the cake, the mind turns nasty.

At this point, the thoughts generated by the mind and the feelings triggered by believing those thoughts normally intensify. If you believe these thoughts, the painful emotions become even stronger than before. The mind may then suggest, 'You may as well give up on losing weight. It's pointless. You'll never get there. You may as well have another piece of cake.' If we are not mindful, this path can lead to eating the whole cake in one night, returning to the fridge again and again, then hating ourselves the next day – which means believing hateful thoughts generated by the mind.

Keep in mind that this example just demonstrates the process, while the content of each person's thoughts may differ. *Your* mind might not be interested in binge eating. Instead, it may tell you to open a bottle of wine, or it might berate you for calling in sick, even though you are bedridden. The content is not as important as understanding the ridiculous nature of the process.

Imagine if your boss told you to do something and then yelled at you for following their instructions. You would start looking for a new job pretty quickly, and you would probably not take much notice of your boss – perhaps even thinking they were a bit crazy. But our minds repeat this behaviour again and again, and time after time we turn to our minds for advice. Why? The problem is that most of us think that the voice in our heads is actually *us*, which is why we say, 'I think...' or 'I want to...'. We identify with each thought, believing that we 'thought' it, but if you watch closely you will see that thoughts come and go with no rhyme or reason. They are completely beyond our control. This is clearly seen when something 'bad' is happening to us and we try not to think about it. In spite of our efforts, the mind dwells on the events, replaying the past and predicting the future. If we had control of our thoughts, we would simply switch them off at these times, but this just isn't possible. We cannot control thoughts, but we can learn not to believe them or be bothered by them, as you will see later in the book.

The bottom line is that if we don't believe the spin of the mind, no negative emotion will arise. Any time we feel fear, stress, anxiety or any other painful emotion, we are believing a thought, even if we aren't consciously aware of it. The great thing is that these feelings can't *actually* hurt us, even though they seem scary at the time. In fact, these emotions can assist us on the path to peace and happiness by showing us what thoughts we still believe and by giving us the opportunity to fully accept them as part of our experience of the present moment. If you don't want to accept them, that's OK, but they will still be there, and unfortunately the things we sometimes do to escape our feelings usually lead to even more negative feelings.

Avoidance behaviour has been shown to increase the intensity of painful feelings over the long term, as well as reducing our ability to cope with those feelings when they do arise; so, what can we do instead? This will be addressed in depth in a later chapter, but for now, let me say that fighting against a feeling gives energy to that feeling; the struggle to get rid of an emotion makes it stronger, just as an angry person becomes louder and more out of control if we yell at them to calm down. Emotions can't sustain themselves without this struggle, without us feeding them by dwelling on events associated with them and listening to the mind's hard-luck stories. If we can sit and pay attention to an emotion without fighting it or feeding it by getting lost in thoughts about 'what happened' to cause it, that emotion will eventually seem to disappear. It is a law of the universe that energy can never vanish altogether, it can only change form, so that negative emotional energy must shift and become something else. I don't know what it becomes, and it really doesn't matter, but I do know that the only way to be free of painful emotions is to learn to sit and observe them – to be still with them. Until we can do this, our lives are run by emotions, and we are tossed this way and that as we seek positive feelings and try to avoid the feelings we dislike. Becoming a whole person involves making friends with these feelings, which we will see are not scary, vicious demons, but no more than scared little children.

The Paradox of Control

Most of us want to control our emotions in order to make life more pleasant, but this is not actually possible.

I call this the 'paradox of control', which basically means that when we try to control our emotions, they become power*ful*, but if we don't try to control them and experience them instead, they become power*less*. So the paradox is that when we try to control an emotion by attempting to change it or escape it, the emotion controls us. We drink to avoid feeling lonely, yell at someone to try to escape our fear and anger, or we eat to get rid of our feelings of worthlessness. We don't actually want to do any of these things, but the desire to escape these emotions drives us to do them, which is why I say our emotions are controlling us. The alternative is to observe these emotions, to be mindful of them, without getting lost in them. This puts us back in control of our behaviour because, without the fear of these emotions, there is no need to do anything to get rid of them, and we can do what we truly want to do. Regardless of our anxiety, we can still go to that new class, talk to that person at the party or go for that job we really want. Without our deep-seated fear of our feelings, life becomes free and easy, with endless possibilities opening up.

Trying to control our feelings gives them power, while allowing them to be as they are brings freedom.

To finish the chapter, let's look at both ways of relating to thoughts and feelings with an example.

Scenario One: Believing Thoughts and Running From Feelings

Imagine you arrive at work and your boss yells at you for losing a big contract. Your mind starts telling you stories like, 'This always happens to you because you're useless, hopeless, and no one could ever love you.' You feel embarrassed and worthless, and a strong fear of rejection and abandonment – which you have suppressed since childhood – arises in you. Your mind then says, 'You'll get fired, you might as well quit', and you run out of the office, seemingly running from the situation, but actually running from your feelings – which, unfortunately, follow you all the way home. So, what happens next? I don't know, but this example shows how painful and confusing life becomes when we believe our thoughts and are afraid of our feelings. The second and third parts of this book are dedicated to the alternative course of action in life: the path of mindfulness, but let's take a glimpse at that right now.

Scenario Two: Mindfulness in Action

You get to work and your boss yells at you for losing a big contract. Your mind, as usual, starts telling you the same old stories. You notice that you believe some of the stories and that this creates painful feelings within you. You sit quietly, experiencing those feelings fully while watching your mind's attempts to pull your attention back to its stories of worthlessness and victimhood. You enjoy the sensation of sitting at your desk and breathing, and you start your work for the day calmly and efficiently. Occasionally, your attention wanders back to the stories, and the pain this creates alerts you to the fact that you are lost, bringing your awareness back to your life as it happens, now. You decide to give four weeks' notice and look for another job, but there is no trace of anger, fear or self-pity in you. You go home and enjoy your weekend without sparing a thought for your boss or the yelling. You are excited about the new possibilities that have opened up because your boss was kind enough to let you know that you should be working somewhere else.

Notice that in scenario two you do not become some sort of doormat. You become a calm, peaceful, efficient human being who is not upset by a seemingly difficult situation. The experience is learnt from and left where it is, in the past, stored in the mind as a memory, no more. It isn't dragged into the present through complaining to friends, dwelling on the experience or trying to avoid the painful feelings, which are instead used as an opportunity to be more deeply aware of the present moment. This is true acceptance, knowing that *what is* is exactly as it should be and then working with the current situation in an appropriate manner. As you move through the rest of this book, you will see that mindfulness is not something that requires you to become a recluse and live in the forest. It is the natural human way when thoughts and feelings are dealt with in a healthy fashion – nothing special.

In concluding this chapter and this section, let me give you a word of encouragement. The path you are undertaking is the only way to be free of these cycles of pain and suffering. I don't mean to say that the exercises in this book are the only way because there are as many paths as people in this world, but the only way I know of to be free from pain is to be connected to the present moment, which implies not believing thoughts nor running away from your feelings. This path is simple and straight, but the mind is complicated and crooked, so the path seems difficult at times. Read on, and you will see how simple it is to live in the moment. Yes, it takes practice and perseverance, but there is nothing overly complicated in the next two parts of the book. Before we move on though, I invite you to spend a few minutes with the following exercise, which will show you how to make peace with the challenging emotions discussed in this chapter.

Notice Every Feeling

We have already explored the problems caused by losing yourself in emotion. The alternative to this is to be mindful, to sit with that emotion with openness and curiosity, freeing yourself of the need to cover up that emotion through compulsive behaviour. Once you learn this process, it becomes a powerful tool to transform anger and hatred into peace and joy.

1 Sit with your spine straight and breathe mindfully.

2 Take your attention inside and feel your body from within. Notice any tension, physical or emotional, without trying to change or get rid of it.

3 Focus your attention on the feeling; just watch it openly, without judgement.

4 Watch for the mind's commentary about the feeling and, if you get lost in thought, come back to experiencing that feeling, noticing it.

5 Continue this practice for as long as you wish.

6 If no feelings arise, just breathe mindfully and watch for any feelings or tension.

Key Points:

• The most important thing about this exercise is to notice the feelings without reacting, storytelling or getting lost in the mind. If you do get lost, come back to the experience.

- Your mind may tell you that the emotion is too strong, that you can't handle it. Notice this thought as more mental chatter and continue to feel that emotion.

- If an emotion is extremely strong, be gentle with yourself and feel it just as much as you can at the time. If you need a break, that's OK, there is no need to push yourself, just keep returning to that feeling and noticing it as much as you can. Each of us must find our own limits in terms of what we can manage at the time, and this is part of our practice too.

Once you understand this exercise, try doing it periodically to check your emotional state. Any time negativity arises within you, take your attention into that feeling and notice the urge to either run away or react through compulsive behaviour or attacking someone else. Pay attention to the strong resistance to what you are feeling right now. This is true acceptance, to sit with strong, uncomfortable feelings without running away or reacting, and it is the beginning of freedom from emotions.

PART TWO

The Mindful Way

As we leave behind the pain and confusion of a life obsessed with the movements of the mind, let's begin an exploration of life free from that suffering, instead walking the path of mindfulness. This section may appear somewhat theoretical, but the insights that strike you as you read it can be powerful, so try to read it mindfully. You can start by taking note of the mind's objections to the ideas expressed in the coming chapters, objections that may take the form of conscious complaints, of general confusion, or of a less conscious feeling of discomfort. These revelations threaten the mind's control, so resistance is highly likely. Try to notice that resistance without either fighting it or getting lost in it. Just observe it and read on.

CHAPTER FIVE

Life without Stories

Mental storytelling is such a part of life that the idea of living without these stories, without listening to our thoughts, can seem strange or even frightening. The assumption behind this fear is that without those stories, we wouldn't be able to function effectively in this world, but is this really the case? Over the course of this chapter, we will examine what life might look like without the endless storytelling and how it is possible to function on a day-to-day basis without listening to our thoughts. This idea may seem alien to you, but it is an invitation to ask the question:

What would happen if I didn't believe my thoughts?

Life without stories, or without believing stories, may seem a strange, or even daunting prospect at first. Most of us are so attached to our stories, especially those related to our self-identity, that the idea of losing them may seem scary, or just plain unimaginable. We have already seen that believing thoughts is a source of pain, and that life without stories is painless and peaceful. I write this from experience because I know how quiet and enjoyable life is when I don't believe my thoughts, as much as I know the pain, confusion and entanglement that occur when I get lost in them. I would like to open this section with an exploration of some of the qualities of a mindful life, starting with 'acceptance'.

Acceptance

Acceptance means learning to see things as they really are instead of viewing them through our preconceived ideas and thoughts. We normally judge thoughts, feelings, events and people as either 'good' or 'bad', a process that happens quickly, and often subconsciously. Practising mindfulness is a chance to become aware of these judgements and to experience life with interest, learning to notice instead of judge. So, when we practise mindfulness of emotions, for example, we sit with emotions and explore them curiously with an open mind. We practise setting aside judgements and instead feel what the emotion is really like. This sounds very abstract in a written format, but it is a concrete practice. When we sit down to practise, we stop trying to control our experiences, we stop trying to get rid of the 'bad' thoughts and emotions and grab on to the 'good' ones. We become the observer of these things, allowing them to come and go, allowing so-called good and so-called bad to be a part of our experience. When we do this, we can finally stop struggling with thoughts and feelings, which means that we can also stop struggling with the events of our lives. To stop struggling does not mean doing nothing to change our circumstances, it just means *accepting* things as they are now.

It is a common misconception that acceptance means doing nothing or becoming some kind of vegetable. Many people see acceptance as a passive quality possessed by hippies and doormats, but what we are talking about is only acceptance of the situation *right now*; you cannot accept the future, as it doesn't exist yet.

Resistance vs Acceptance

Let's say you are completely broke, without a dollar to your name. The normal reaction would be what I would call 'resistance', which might involve feeling scared and angry, listening to stories of victimhood or of the gloomy, scary future told to you by the mind, and generally feeling sorry for yourself. In this type of situation, people think acceptance means sitting down and saying, 'Oh well, I don't have any money. That's all right. I'll just wait here until someone comes to rescue me.' This is not acceptance, it is believing the story that 'there's nothing I can do.' Acceptance might look like this: you check your bank account and see that you have no money. Realising that the rent is due, you talk to your landlord about options, or ask a friend to lend you some money. Once the immediate situation is dealt with, you consider what caused the situation and make changes, if possible, in order to better manage your money. You do all of these things without fear, guilt, anger or resentment, enjoying each moment and noticing the good things that happened because you didn't have money. You got to go for a walk instead of driving, you got to know your nice landlord better, and you got to have a cup of tea with a dear friend, who was more than happy to lend you some money. 'Acceptance' should not be confused with believing a 'story of acceptance', because it is beyond thinking. Acceptance is what happens when you don't believe the mind's painful stories about the situation.

The Dalai Lama is a great example of true acceptance, having gone through incredible hardship, yet being able to accept what has happened without anger or resentment. Does this mean that he doesn't act to try and improve conditions for his people? Clearly it doesn't. The Dalai Lama spends his life travelling to spread peace and to raise awareness of the plight of his people, but he does this in a peaceful way, winning many supporters along the way. If he were an angry crusader chanting about the evils of China, I think the

Dalai Lama would be viewed very differently by the world. There are countless other examples of people who have been able to accept difficult circumstances, then work ceaselessly to change them, but the most important thing to consider is how to practise acceptance in our own lives. Luckily, it is simple and we don't need a university degree to start practising – in fact, you can start right now! Start by breathing mindfully, that is, becoming aware of your breathing, really feeling it. Allow your breathing to be natural, accept it, long or short, deep or shallow. As you breathe mindfully, you may notice thoughts arising in your mind. Take notice of these thoughts, and notice the mind's complaining, its resistance to life as it is. Becoming aware of resistance without engaging in it is acceptance in itself.

There are many things in life that our minds don't like – housework, work, pain, sickness and talking to people we don't like are just a few examples. When the mind doesn't like something, it tells us a thousand stories in an effort to avoid experiencing that particular thing. When we believe these stories, we experience life through the prism of the mind, which colours and shapes our experiences. So it may be that we have never experienced just doing the housework, we have only experienced the housework accompanied by the mind's stories about doing the housework, like being at a lively festival while listening to a cynical editorial about it.

Many people have never experienced doing

housework without the mind's running commentary, and therefore they believe it to be an onerous task. However, what is the difference between walking along with the vacuum and walking the dog? The difference is in the mind. If you can accept vacuuming instead of resisting it, you can enjoy it for what it is, without the story that 'before I was sitting on the couch and now I am vacuuming (which sucks). I hope I can finish quickly so I can do something more enjoyable!' Listening to the story is what creates the unpleasant feelings associated with vacuuming, which is enjoyable when experienced moment-to-moment, without trying to get through it, on to the next thing. The same goes for any so-called 'chore'.

It is easy to confuse acceptance with thinking positively about things we usually don't like, putting on a brave face if you will. For example, you might try to 'accept' a painful situation, like someone dying, by rationalising it, even finding the positives in it. This could include trying to believe thoughts like, 'He's better off now, he's not in pain anymore.' This is what we usually call acceptance, but what we are examining in this chapter, which I call 'mindful acceptance', does not involve thinking, it involves experiencing the events of your everyday life without believing the mind's commentary. So, when painful thoughts about a situation start to arise, mindful acceptance means accepting those thoughts too, allowing them to be there without getting lost in them. Notice those thoughts, be aware of them and, if you get lost in them, bring your attention back to the present. This is true acceptance. In the case of someone dying, acceptance includes experiencing painful emotions, noticing our painful thoughts about the situation, and taking action when it becomes appropriate. What we stop doing is getting lost in stories about the past and the future, such as 'I can't live without him.' When we allow the experience to happen, to be as it is without getting lost in our stories, we can be peaceful even in these extreme circumstances.

The most important thing is to know that thoughts are not the truth, nor do they represent the world as it is, they are just stories about reality. When we watch our thoughts, aware that they are merely stories, we can more easily accept all parts of our experience.

Anything we fear or resent doing, we are resisting, but don't take my word for it. Start to take notice of the stories your mind is telling you whenever you feel negative about something. Awareness of these stories opens the door to something new. Once we accept things in this way, they lose the power to make us unhappy, and our happiness no longer depends on external events. This is true freedom, and it is available for you now just by noticing your life, your thoughts and the mind's resistance. If this doesn't make sense yet, don't worry. Just keep bringing your attention back to this moment. This is all that is necessary.

Simplicity

The world we live in is becoming more complex every day. If you are sceptical about this, take a trip to the supermarket where even buying toilet paper can become a confusing ordeal for the unprepared. It is the same when it comes to information, with reams written on every subject available at the click of a mouse, leaving people overloaded, with no idea of the actual quality of the information presented. Our lives can become like this too. If we are not careful, we can end up with houses, calendars and minds full of stuff, most of it utterly useless. We can find ourselves so carried away by the events of our lives that life itself gets lost; we stop experiencing life as it is happening. Mindfulness is the antidote to this. Under normal circumstances, it seems that to have a good life, we need many exciting things to happen: we need to win the lottery, we need to go on holiday to Bali, we need our team to win, etc. Excitement is fine, but when we make having as many pleasurable or exciting experiences as possible the main focus of our lives, something goes awry. It is like having chocolate for breakfast. Once is fine, but if you do it every day, it becomes a problem. In the same way, if we live for excitement, our lives lose their depth as each short high is immediately followed by a low, then the search for more excitement. I am not talking about drug-induced highs here, but the effect is similar. We build up so much anticipation around an event that it either doesn't live up to our expectations or we feel depressed afterwards, sad that it is over. We can carry this feeling for a long time, thinking, 'I felt so good then. If only I could get back to that.'

When we practise mindfulness, we set all this aside and learn to enjoy quiet simplicity. Sitting and breathing doesn't sound that exciting, and really it isn't. Nevertheless, when we sit and just breathe, just observe the breath, the body and the sights and sounds around us, a deeper enjoyment arises. The stillness that comes when the mind becomes quiet – or at least less noisy – is incredibly peaceful and joyful. Practising mindfulness, we learn that this joy is always with us but incessant mental activity obscures it. We learn to enjoy the simplicity of life, of sitting, walking, breathing. None of it will make the news: 'Man sits in chair, breathes. More details to follow.' But, in fact, simplicity is the heart of our lives. I don't think that life without breathing, without eating, without going to the toilet would be too enjoyable, but our minds are not interested in the simple things. Instead, we set out to accomplish grand plans, ignoring simplicity, awareness and peace. These plans, goals and endeavours are great, but they are made up of a string of simple moments, small steps. It is easy to get so caught up in a big idea that the steps along the way get ignored, but actually our entire lives are made up of small steps. Our whole lives are now, this one breath. When we walk, we focus on each step, one at a time. When we take each step, we treat it as the only step that exists. When we breathe, we notice the qualities of each breath, and we find peace in this intense, aware noticing. In Zen, there is great emphasis on paying attention to detail, on doing things with care and attention. This is the attitude we take into mindfulness practice; we learn to notice the details of each moment, to slow down enough to see the beauty all around us. Focusing on each step in isolation, the mind naturally slows down, and when the mind slows down, the world seems to slow down with it. This is the return of peace, of awareness, and it is available each moment, no matter what is happening in the outside world.

Freedom from Problems

When living mindfully, we are naturally free from problems, which exist only in the mind. This doesn't mean that challenging events will not happen, but problems are basically believed thoughts about these situations, not the situations themselves. If your partner leaves you, the world would call this a problem, but it is only problematic if you listen to the mind's stories about the past and future such as: 'In the past, I had a partner, which was good, but now I'm so lonely, and I might never find someone else. I'm not getting any younger after all.' The problem is the actual thinking itself, without which you could accept the situation. Without referring to the past, there is only the present situation, which is 'I don't have a partner.' Acceptance of that might lead you in many different directions. You might catch up with old friends now that you have more time alone, you might go to that place you always wanted to visit but never got around to, or you might just continue living your life as it is, free of the pain created by listening to the stories in your mind. This could include looking for a new partner, reconciling with your ex-partner or staying single. *What* we do is less important than the way we approach each moment and *how* we do things. Choosing to do things with care and attention, rather than with haste and distraction, lost in stories. This is what determines the quality of our lives. This morning, before I sat down to write this, my eight-month-old son was coughing continuously, the result of some sort of virus he picked up recently. To give my wife a break, I walked around the lounge trying to help him sleep, rocking him on my shoulder while he slept fitfully, interrupted by his cough. As I walked back and forth with him, almost no thoughts arose in my mind, and those that did arise were not listened to. Because of this, I was completely calm and peaceful, although this didn't stop me from doing whatever was possible to help my son. There was no problem being created in my mind, just peace and quiet. I am not some enlightened guru, I am an ordinary, everyday person just like you, and the peace I am describing is there for anyone who can stop believing their painful thoughts by bringing their attention into this moment. You can live like this too. The following exercise is a powerful, simple way to develop this kind of attention, by carefully listening to each sound as it arises. Take a few minutes to dive into this wonderful practice.

Notice Every Sound

1 Sit still for a moment and take a few mindful breaths.

2 As you continue to breathe mindfully, pay attention to what you can hear – both inside and outside.

3 Listen to each sound intently, without judgement. If judgements arise, simply notice them while staying focused on the sounds around you.

4 Spend a few minutes just listening without getting lost in thought. Listen as intently as possible, allowing each sound to come and go.

Key Points:

• By listening without excessive thinking, you can fully experience each sound. Whether your mind considers the sounds beautiful or ugly is unimportant; what matters is your undivided attention, so be as alert as you can.

• This is a powerful activity to try when listening to another person. Try listening carefully to each word they say without paying attention to the mind's running commentary. People may surprise you with their wisdom and insight.

• Try it now. Put on a favourite piece of music, or, if you are out, put the book down for a few minutes and notice every sound you can hear around you.

CHAPTER SIX

The Essence of Mindfulness

The essence of mindfulness is to be totally in the moment with openness and interest instead of getting lost in the judgements of the mind. Living in the present brings freedom from pain through freedom from time, as suffering cannot be created without referring to the past and the future.

Freedom from Time

When we think of life, we usually think of 'my life', which is basically a story that we must keep telling ourselves in order to keep it alive. If we watch the story or listen closely to the mind telling it over and over, we will soon get bored with it. 'My life' will become dull and uninteresting. Identified with the mind and lost in thoughts, we must continue to create drama, find problems to solve and change things in order to have something to talk and think about. Without this, we feel great emptiness, we feel as if 'life is passing me by'. This statement shows that 'me' and 'life' are considered separate, but how can this be? How can you be separate from your life? This story exists in the mind, which imagines a stream of time running from past to future, with *me* as the central character in the story. This brings with it feelings of insecurity because we know that this stream leads eventually to death, of which the mind is petrified. But does time as we know it actually exist? Of course, time is real in the sense that we have a standard measure to track the changing of the seasons, the rising and setting of the sun, and the ageing of the body. This is time in a practical sense, and it helps us to function as a species, but the time with which the human mind is obsessed exists only in our heads. Human beings are lost in the past and scared of the future, spending more time thinking about yesterday and tomorrow than experiencing the present. But where are the past and future located? Where can they be found? The past is a memory, which is happening now; the future is a projection of what will happen, which is happening now, and in the middle we have the present, which actually is happening now. So, where are we all this time? Or we might ask *when* are we? Now, of course!

Now is the only time, and life in this moment is the only life. Everything else is imaginary, it is a thought, an idea, a concept. There is no problem with it, so why worry about it? When we give more attention to the past and future, forsaking the present, we divide ourselves because we can only ever be *here now*, but we are trying to be *there then*. Our legs are walking to work while the rest of our body is trying to catch the bus! No wonder life is so exhausting! We are trying to control the past, which is gone, and the future, which will be as it will be. This attempted control is completely futile, so why do we focus on the past and the future when we can only be in the here and now? The thinking mind can only be engaged in the past and future because the mind uses analytical processes. It calculates and considers life, but it cannot directly experience life. In order to analyse something, it must have already happened, it has to be a finished event. You cannot think about something in real time because there is always a delay, which is why to be good at activities like sport, the mind must not be relied upon – it is always a step behind. The thinking mind can analyse the past and project into the future, which is a useful skill in many situations because it allows us to learn from mistakes and to plan ahead. Even though our analysis of the past is often biased, and our plans don't usually come out as expected, we can use this function without causing problems if we are clear that the thinking mind is merely a tool for dealing with the past and future. These are the only things it knows, and when we become attached to the thoughts and ideas generated by the thinking mind, confusion arises. We get lost in thoughts that cannot be in real time, so it is only natural that we are obsessed with the past and the future.

Because of this obsession with time, and the mind's fear of death, we constantly try to foresee the future to figure out how things will work out for us.

We all know deep down that each life form dies in the end, so we experience uneasiness, particularly as death approaches. This uneasiness can be seen by comparing a five-year-old to an eighty-year-old – although it is not true of everyone. It drives us to try and predict exactly how things will turn out so we can feel comfortable and secure. As we become ever more interested in the obviously uncertain future, we turn to the past to help us predict what will happen. When we live in this way, we can end up treating life like a minefield, constantly looking ahead to see where we should step. To the mind, this makes perfect sense, but it also leaves us in a state of uneasiness and anxiety, and it limits our capacity to enjoy things as they are happening. The conundrum is that until we stop worrying about how things will turn out, we can never feel at ease and secure in a deep and lasting way, which has many implications for our happiness. The fact that we turn to past memories for fulfilment shows that we are not satisfied with now, and the fact that we look for a happy future shows that we are not happy now.

The result of trying to find happiness in the future is that we are always straining to get there quickly, believing that it will be better than now. Therefore, we feel anxious and rushed all the time, yet we never seem to get anywhere. Life becomes a struggle and we are miserable. This misery increases after each thing we thought would make us happy appears and doesn't fulfil us, until we have done everything that the world tells us should make us happy, but still we feel incomplete.

As people get older, the hope of happiness in the future becomes less believable, and many people become withdrawn and depressed, especially in cultures like ours that deny the value of anything 'old'. When the future looks grim, we can be driven to look at the present moment, especially if the past wasn't that great either. Once we have discovered that none of the world's 'achievements' bring lasting happiness, we have the opportunity to give up, to feel hopeless and think, 'What is the point?' I remember sitting on a hill one day close to tears because everything was going well in my life but I still felt miserable. I sat there and asked myself, 'What is the meaning of it all? You can gain things and make money, but then you die, so why bother? What's the point?' Out of this deep sense of frustration and misery, I eventually discovered something that had been with me all along. That 'something' was life at this moment. So the way to escape from the misery of being trapped in a story is to live in real time, to bring your attention into this moment. This is what we do in mindfulness: we settle into the moment, into ourselves. We simply sit and breathe, engaged in the practice here and now. Each time our attention slides away from the here and now, we return to the breath, we sit up straight and we come back to the moment. This seems unremarkable, and the Zen masters tell us that it is nothing special, which is why the mind dislikes it. The mind wants to feel special, and sitting and breathing is the most *un*special thing in the universe. Imagine you ask your friend to go to a nightclub, and he says, 'Actually I'm going to sit quietly tonight and breathe. Do you want to join me?' Which sounds more interesting, more exciting? Thus it can seem that meditation is a waste of time, but the truth is that until we become aware, until we can be here right now, everything is ultimately meaningless, which is why just sitting is such a beautiful thing to do.

When we are mindful, we are free from time in the sense that we stop focusing on the thoughts about the past and future in our minds. If we go into this state of timelessness for even a few moments, we will notice that life seems very simple all of a sudden. Without the layers of complexity added by listening to the mind, life is quiet and peaceful. This is not something mystical or magical, it is just life as it is now, and you can experience it just by bringing your attention into the present. So, what might this look like in your life?

Mindfulness in Action

Without obsessing about the future, we can enjoy each experience life brings us without striving to get to the future, which will arrive in its own good time anyway. This means that every activity becomes enjoyable and meaningful, regardless of what the mind may tell us, and that peace becomes our companion – even in challenging situations. When we stop wasting energy thinking about the future – apart from when necessary – we naturally have more energy to devote to our lives, and the drudgery and resistance created by the mind's desire to get away from this moment are replaced by interest, curiosity and joy. It is a bit like being a child again: interested in everything we come across, enjoying each experience as if we have never done it before. Why is it that a child can go to the same park every day without getting 'bored'? The mind will tell us that they lack the intelligence for this to happen, but the truth is that children understand something the rest of us have forgotten: every trip to the park is different. This trip to the park is not the same as yesterday's. There may be different people there, and we will do different things, even if they appear the same. Children don't consciously think this of course, they just don't know any different because they aren't yet totally lost in the mind's chatter, in thoughts about the past and future.

When we begin to live more and more in this state of connectedness to the moment, there is more joy and laughter than before. Problems that previously would have seemed dire, desperate or scary, now seem unimportant. If we can do something about them, we do it. If not, we leave them alone and focus on enjoying life instead. This brings freedom from the worry and stress created by listening to the mind's scary futuristic tales, which rarely turn out as the mind anticipated anyway. Relationships become easier as we allow other people to be as they are without trying to control their behaviour through manipulation. Someone can appear to hate us, and this is OK because without time, our imagined self-image isn't so important. That self-image is a bundle of thoughts about the past that cannot affect life now. Without that sense of time, the need for security diminishes. Although we still look for food and shelter, the need to *feel* secure, to believe a story of security, disappears. In truth, the mind never feels secure, at least not for long because it sees threats everywhere, hence the money spent on armed forces around the world.

At any time, the things the mind identifies with, like our house, our car, our job, our friends or our social position, could disappear. The house burns down, the car is stolen, our job is cut and our friends turn on us. If all this happened in one day, most of us would collapse in a heap. We invest so much energy in trying to get and maintain all these things that losing them is almost like death to the mind. However, if we are mindful, living in the present, there is only what is in front of us now. So, unless we are in the car, the car isn't a part of our experience now, it isn't too important. This doesn't mean we will forget to pay the insurance premiums, it just means we aren't wasting our lives worrying about losing these things, or grieving over them when they go. Life is a constant process of birth and death, with death needed to bring something new into the world, to create space for exciting changes. If our car is stolen, for example, we may have to ride our bike, which might help us get fit, strong and healthy, and it could turn out to be the best thing that ever happened. Losing our job creates the opportunity for something new to arise, possibly something more wonderful than we ever imagined. Freedom from time means freedom from thoughts, and this is the only real security available to us. It offers security not based on external, unstable things, but based on this moment, which has always been with us and will always stay with us. To experience this moment fully, I invite you to spend some time experiencing the sights and sounds around you. This practice can bring joy and vitality into the everyday activities that the mind would rather ignore. Living this freedom is your birthright, so read on and enjoy.

Noticing the Senses

Awareness of sense perception is a powerful meditative tool. The senses are with us all the time, and paying attention to them pulls our awareness into the present. Try the following exercise, spending a few minutes gradually expanding your awareness of your senses.

1 Sit down and breathe mindfully for five breaths with your eyes closed.

2 After the fifth breath, pay attention to the sounds you can hear, noticing every different sound.

3 Open your eyes and notice what you can see, such as the light and shade, the objects around you and their colour.

4 Stand up, and notice what that feels like. Notice the way your feet make contact with the ground and the way your shoulders rise and fall. See if you can feel your heart beating.

5 Take in as much as you can for at least a minute.

6 Try it now, and if you get distracted by a thought, notice that you have drifted away and bring your attention back to the exercise.

CHAPTER SEVEN

Unconditional Happiness

Is it possible to be happy, to be at peace, regardless of our external circumstances? The mind would say no, but the truth is a little different. In this chapter, we will look at the accepted view of happiness, which I call 'conditional happiness', and the role it plays in the suffering humans experience. We will also examine what I call the 'structure of suffering', that is, how we create our own suffering in the first place. These ideas may seem radical or unbelievable, and your mind may make unfavourable comments about them. If this happens, try to notice what your mind is saying, take a mindful breath and then return your attention to the text. Try to see the examples as your examples, even though they may not be things you have done. It is easy to see what other people are doing to create suffering, but through seeing how you are creating your own suffering right now, you can find freedom, so read on with openness and curiosity.

What Is Conditional Happiness?

If I were to put it into one sentence, I would say that conditional happiness means believing that we need something other than what we have in order to be happy – putting conditions on our happiness. This is what the Buddha called 'delusion', believing our thoughts about how the world needs to change in order to accommodate our preferences so we can be happy. The reason I said in the introduction that the idea of having no conditions on our happiness is revolutionary is because our view of the world for our whole lives is that things need to change before we can be happy. These 'things' may be external things, such as your job, your financial situation, your partner (or lack of) or some other aspect of external life. They may also be internal things, like your thoughts, feelings and emotions. The mind examines these things, labels them as 'good' or 'bad', and then sets about its task: getting rid of the bad and increasing the good. Actually, these labels of good and bad are just our opinions, but we treat them as indisputable facts, and if someone dares to have a different opinion, conflict is often the result.

Let's look at this in more detail with an example of conditional happiness. Imagine that you are single, feeling lonely and depressed. The thought that 'I need a partner. If only I had a partner I would be happy' continually repeats itself in your mind, and each time you believe it to be a concrete fact. When you tell the story that 'I need a partner' to others, they are sympathetic and they confirm your story, trying to reassure you: 'Don't worry, you'll find someone eventually', but the thoughts and the pain remain. Believing that you need a partner in order to be happy and that you may never find one (a thought that provokes fear and anxiety), you suffer, convinced that the missing ingredient for your happiness is your knight in shining armour. This is a common fairy tale. Imagine that you find a partner and, for a while, everything seems right. You move in together, but, after a few months, cracks appear in the relationship. Your partner's faults become more obvious and new thoughts appear: 'If only he were more..., I wish he didn't..., Why does he have to...?' Again, happiness eludes you, but now it appears that your partner is at fault, and unless you have the insight to see that the problem lies not in the situation, but in the thoughts you are believing, you may react angrily toward your partner, believing *they* need to change in order for *you* to be happy. This is the normal way humans seek happiness, but it simply never works. The main problem with this way of living is that it leads to constant conflict because life never (or rarely) conforms to our wishes. This leaves us with two options: To accept life as it is and respond to it as well as we can, or to argue, fight, complain and struggle, spending time and energy thinking about why things should be different.

Accepting life as it is doesn't mean rolling over and waiting for things to change. We can still be active in trying to improve our lives, but do the struggle, anger and frustration help us make those changes? No. This struggle simply wastes energy and ensures that we will never be happy because we have placed conditions on that happiness. Arguing with reality is a no-win situation, as you may have already discovered. It isn't possible to change reality as it is now, in this moment. Right now, everything is exactly as it is. This point really cannot be argued, but we argue nonetheless. We think that other people should be nice to us, that politicians should do as we wish, that it shouldn't rain on our wedding day – but it still does. Believing these untrue thoughts leaves us angry and frustrated, complaining to anyone who will listen. This is highly ineffective, but it is what almost everyone does.

So, what is the alternative? We will look at that in a moment, but first, let's have a look at how we create suffering in the first place.

The Structure of Suffering

When I say the 'structure of suffering', what I mean is the way we create suffering for ourselves. In a way, this has already been explained in the previous section because suffering occurs when there is a gap between what we have and what we want. Western psychology has recently recognised this, but most psychological frameworks try to close that gap by getting more of what we want, or by changing our thinking and 're-storying' to make reality more palatable. Some re-storying almost resembles an attempt to trick ourselves into believing a different, more pleasant story, while the other approach, that of trying to make reality change to suit our desires, is what we are already doing anyway. This struggle merely creates stress and suffering as we fight with reality, sure that we know how things should be ... but do we really? Living mindfully, we don't assume that we know how the world should look, instead we become curious and inquisitive, and we experience life as it is.

When we have something but we believe we should have something else, we suffer. When our partner is silent and we believe they should be talking to us, we suffer. There are two ways to close this gap. The first is to struggle with reality, and good luck to you if it works. The second has many names, but here I call it 'unconditional happiness.'

What Is Unconditional Happiness?

Unconditional happiness means exactly what it says: no longer putting conditions on our happiness. It also means opening our minds to the possibility that we can be happy here, now, without anything in our lives needing to change. This state can also be called mindfulness, or simply living in the present moment – they are basically the same. Let me start with a question: What would your life be like right now if you didn't believe that you needed anything to be different? If you didn't believe the thoughts about what your life is lacking? Let's return to our previous example to examine this in more detail.

Picture yourself again living alone, without a partner. Your friends feel very sorry for you because everyone knows that it is better to have a partner ... or is it? You, however, live in a state of acceptance, free from painful beliefs about what should be different in your life. Instead of complaining and living in a state of angry resistance, you live in a state of mindfulness, anchored in the present moment. Fearful thoughts about a solitary future rarely occur to you, and when they do, you refuse to get lost in them, you simply watch them come and go. This leaves you free to fully experience the life you are living instead of wishing for something different to come along. Life is so rich and full that you simply cannot believe you need another person there to complete you, or that anything is missing. If you meet someone, great. If not, that's good too. Whatever happens, you live in a state of peace, enjoying everything that comes your way.

So, which way would you prefer: struggle and resistance or peace and acceptance? In the second scenario, you might be more likely to meet someone as you continue living your life happily and peacefully. People are naturally attracted to other people living in this way. In contrast, living in a stressful, resistant way may reduce your chances of meeting that perfect partner. In fact, that person could be right in front of you, but how would you notice when your attention is absorbed by painful, scary thoughts about the past and the future? However, whether you meet that person or remain single for the rest of your life, you can live peacefully and happily. When we live in this way, a partner is an added bonus, which means that we don't need them to do certain things – like stay with us or be nice to us all the time – to make us happy. This leaves them free to live their own life, and we get to go along for the ride. This is incredibly freeing for a relationship

Mindfulness in Action

When we practise mindfulness, we sit and accept whatever arises. We stay anchored in the moment, whatever thoughts and emotions come along. We learn to notice the rhythm of our breathing, the senses and the sights and sounds around us, even in the midst of great confusion and mental activity. We learn to integrate these external and internal happenings into our awareness, which keeps expanding to include everything. In practice, this means that whatever arises, in our meditation as well as in our lives, we continually return our attention to the body, the breath and the senses. Any time we get lost in our thoughts, our feelings, or in arguing with what is happening, we keep coming back to this moment, which is all we ever have.

if you can do it, but it takes awareness of your reactions and resistance. The more we can live and allow others to live as they wish, the more we are free to enjoy our lives. This is where mindfulness practice starts to ripen, when it permeates every area of our lives.

For example, imagine that after a great night's sleep and a wonderful breakfast with your family, you walk outside to go to work. Standing in the driveway, you look around in disbelief as you notice that your car isn't there. You think back to the night before and remember parking it in the driveway, which leaves only one explanation: it has been stolen. Your mind begins to race, your emotions threaten to explode and then you remember your practice and take a mindful breath. You use the rising emotions as part of your practice by observing the physical sensations of them rising in your chest and stomach. You bring a curious openness to these sensations, allowing them to be there without a struggle. You notice thoughts like, 'I should have checked the steering lock...', 'I won't be able to get to work', without believing them or fighting them. You calmly assess your options, call the police and then call work. You go back inside to wait for the police and explain to your partner what has happened. You both have a laugh and enjoy this unexpected time together. The police arrive, and you make a report before taking the train to work. Arriving at work, you have a bit of a laugh about the whole situation before getting into what you have to do for the day. If painful thoughts or feelings about the situation come along, you use them as part of your practice and become aware of them without getting lost. If you do get lost, you use your breath to return your attention to the present moment. You leave looking for the car to the police and take care of your own life with peace and joy. Will the car be found? Maybe yes, maybe no. Either way, you continue to return to *now*, using whatever opportunities life provides to strengthen your practice. Let me ask a question: Does responding in this way reduce your chances of getting your car back, or make your life worse in any way? Your mind may say that it reduces the chances of getting the car back, that you need to fight and struggle to fix things, but is that really true? Try it next time some supposed misfortune befalls you. You may be surprised by the result.

When we act with mindfulness, life becomes much more simple, straightforward and enjoyable. We don't need much to be content, and we don't waste time and energy dwelling on the past or worrying about the future. We take responsibility for our inner world instead of focusing on and trying to manipulate the outer world. When we become aware of having deviated from this path, we return to it and notice what thoughts we got lost in. Our awareness of this moment becomes more important than whether we get what we want or not, and we are free to enjoy so-called 'success' as well as 'failure'.

What conditions are you putting on your happiness?

Complete the following sentences and write a list of your mind's demands.

In order to be happy, I need _____.

It is impossible to be happy right now because

_____.

If only I had more _____ then I would be happy.

If only I hadn't _____, then I would be happy.

When _____ I will be happy.

Seeing the mind's demands on paper can be an interesting process, and your list might say something like:

In order to be happy, I need a house, a better job, a partner and a boss who is nice to me. I need my kids to behave themselves and to try hard at school, and I need the world to become a more peaceful place.

What do you believe you need in order to be happy and at peace? Read these demands carefully. They are the barriers that stand between you and peace, contentment and happiness. Go inside yourself for a moment and notice where the unhappiness, the angst, is occurring. Does it come from the outside world, or is it happening in your mind? If the pain, suffering and resentment are happening inside, then your mind is creating it. This is very good news. You are creating your own disease, which means that you can also stop creating it right now. Of course, the pain will take some time to dissipate, but you can stop creating more pain when you no longer believe your thoughts. You can't do this by simply trying not to believe them; in my experience that doesn't work. Instead, deepen your practice of paying attention to the present moment.

Every exercise in this book is designed to draw your attention into the present, and you can continue that journey right now by taking notice of the thoughts that pass through your mind, starting to watch them, and maintaining mindfulness in this moment. Thoughts have no power when we are connected to now, and without the painful, stressful thoughts, would that unhappiness remain? If the answer is no, then the truth is clear. Believing our thoughts is the only thing standing between ourselves and happiness.

On our journey so far, we have practised some simple exercises that can easily be incorporated into everyday life. Now I would like to share in more detail my guide to formal practice – to sitting mindfully. Ten to twenty minutes of this practice, as often as you can manage, will lead to more clarity, peace and alertness in your life. I hope that these guidelines will make your experience of sitting mindfully smooth and enjoyable.

Sitting Mindfully

Sitting meditation is the platform of mindfulness practice, and regular formal sitting practice will give great strength to your day-to-day mindfulness as you live your life. Even doing ten or fifteen minutes a day can help support your awareness as it grows throughout the day. Many people tell me they have no time for this practice. If this would be your response, notice what you choose to do instead, such as watching TV, surfing the internet or reading. I am not saying you should not do these things, just find fifteen minutes between them to practise mindfulness. Here are some basic instructions.

Settling

- Decide how long you will sit for and set a timer – 10–20 minutes is manageable for most people, but feel free to adjust as needed. Setting a timer helps you forget about the clock and concentrate on the practice – simply set the timer, put it where you can't see it and forget about the time altogether.

- Sit down on a chair, the floor, or a meditation cushion, it doesn't matter.

- Get into a comfortable position with your spine

straight. If you are sitting on a chair, try to sit up straight so your back is not leaning against the chair.

- Sitting with a straight back is very important because having a straight spine assists us in staying present in the moment, so check if you are leaning forward or back, left or right and adjust as required.

- If you begin to slouch due to tiredness, take a break from sitting, but try to maintain your awareness of this moment. Stand up, stretch, look around, and come back to sitting when you feel refreshed. Your back muscles will naturally strengthen over time.

The Eyes

- It is fine to sit with your eyes open or closed. If you sit with your eyes open, you may find it helpful to look at the ground in front of you.

- If your eyes are open, allow your vision to be open, that is, do not focus on a particular point but allow your eyes to take in everything in your field of vision.

The Breath

- Every exercise begins with mindful breathing, which involves emptying your lungs as much as you can, then allowing them to fill naturally. Repeat this two or three times to bring your attention back to the moment, then allow your breath to proceed naturally.

- As you do this, pay attention to the physical sensations involved in breathing, like the feeling of your chest expanding and the rise and fall of your shoulders.

- If thoughts or judgements about your breath arise, notice them and then return your attention to the breath.

The Senses

- Expand your awareness to take in your breath and all of your senses. Notice what you can see (if your eyes are open), hear, feel, smell and taste.

- Allow the sensations to float into your awareness without judgement.

- If judgements or comments arise, just notice them and return your attention to your senses.

The Body

- Notice the physical sensations of your body, including emotional energy, tension, heat, cold, etc.

- Again, watch for your mind's commentary, notice the thoughts and judgements, and return your attention to the sensations themselves.

Just Sit

- It sounds easy to 'just sit', but for humans it is incredibly difficult because of the mind's incessant activity.

- Just sitting means sitting and noticing all the things mentioned above, as well as thoughts and feelings, without getting lost in anything.

- When you do get lost, just notice that you are daydreaming and return your attention to your spine, check that it is straight, then notice your breath, your senses and your body.

Rising

- When the alarm goes, have a stretch and slowly get to your feet.

- When you stand up, take your time and remember to be as mindful as you can while you resume your daily activities.

Key Points:

- Focus your attention on what it feels like to breathe.

- Expand your awareness to take in your senses: What can you hear, smell and feel physically?

- Notice what's happening inside – check for stress, tension and any emotions, and observe these sensations without trying to change or get rid of them.

- Notice your thoughts – watch them come and go without getting lost in them.

- Every time you get lost in a thought, bring your attention back to the breath and continue to sit mindfully.

CHAPTER EIGHT

Peace Every Moment

When we are lost in the mind, believing our thoughts and running from our feelings, peace seems far away, something that can only be found in the future if we do all the right things and life goes our way. With so many thoughts obscuring the peace that is already in our lives, it is no wonder that peace seems so unattainable. Luckily, the problem is a simple misunderstanding: we are looking in the wrong place, or, more accurately, the wrong *time*. Peace cannot be found in the future, it can only be found when we stop focusing on the future and sit quietly in this moment.

Mindfulness in Action

Imagine sitting in your car with the engine running. You notice the noise of the engine and, not understanding that the noise comes from the engine, you decide to leave this noisy place and find some peace. As you drive away, the noise seems to follow you, so you drive faster, desperately trying to escape it as you become more and more frantic. You continue to drive around for some time before, in desperation, you ask a peaceful-looking person on the side of the road how you can escape this noisy place. The person smiles knowingly and says, 'Have you thought about turning the car off?'

You consider this for a moment before asking, 'But how would I be able to escape from the noise if I turned the car off? I'd be stuck here.'

The stranger laughs and tells you to try it anyway, you can always turn the car back on if necessary. This makes sense so you do as the stranger suggests. Turning the key back the other way, a deafening silence erupts as the engine cuts out. You laugh at your foolishness, thank the stranger and continue living your life.

When we chase peace in the future, we are doing the same thing. The actual chasing is what prevents us from being peaceful in the first place, but we keep doing it, believing it is the way to find peace. Turning the car off represents mindfulness practice, in which we learn to cut the fuel line to the mind's remembering and projection. The car still runs for a while, but once the lines are empty, it stops and there is quiet. We can still use the car when needed, but we are no longer tormented by its constant noise. This is the mindful life; it is peace every moment.

An End in Itself

If we are to step out of this cycle of chasing some kind of future happiness, we must begin to do things for their own sake, and mindfulness practice is a good starting point for this. Mindfulness is not a means to achieve something, although it leads to many benefits along the way, which are actually more like bonuses. We may experience great peace and joy while practising, but these by-products are not goals to strive for, as striving for goals is incompatible with mindfulness. Striving implies that we have a desire to change something, while mindfulness simply means experiencing the moment as it is, so if we are striving for peace and happiness, we are no longer in a state of mindfulness.

Striving for peace and happiness is like running away from our shadow; there is no way to escape, no matter how fast we run. Mindfulness involves making friends with that shadow, with the parts of ourselves we normally reject.

When we do this, when we make friends with this moment regardless of how it appears, we can sit down and rest, no longer feeling the need to escape. The irony is that by not fighting for peace or chasing happiness, they are there naturally, and that experience of peace and happiness affects everyone we come into contact with in some way. Once we start to live in this state of connectedness with the present moment, the emotions of negativity, like anger and fear, become transformed into peace too.

What I am talking about here I sometimes call 'peace every moment', which means being peaceful, 'being peace', in all situations and circumstances from moment to moment. This really only means being peace now, but let me qualify something. Being peace does not mean no thoughts arise, or that no emotions or emotional reactions arise within. Being peace means accepting our total experience now, and this could include feelings of fear, anger, frustration and pain. Peace means accepting these emotions too, not by telling ourselves stories about them, but by experiencing them, by sitting still and feeling them, by ending our struggle against them.

These emotions can only be sustained and recreated through the process of struggling against them, so ending the struggle is itself peace. I use the term 'peace every moment' because peace is not something we achieve or project into the future. Peace is something that requires our mindfulness to sustain it initially; it needs our awareness and attention to prevent the mind from taking over again, from creating pain and suffering.

Imagine growing a garden in a place where it is sunny every day and rains every night. After planting, we would only need to weed regularly in order to protect the young seedlings. This awareness is like weeding, it is about watching carefully to observe the patterns of the mind, the storytelling and problem making. The more the garden develops, and the more our awareness grows, the less weeding is required. Weeds do not grow in a rainforest, but in a garden they can take over in a matter of weeks. When our attention is anchored in the present, the imagined past and future lose energy, and at the same time, that connectedness to now grows stronger until eventually it seems natural.

Harmony

Peace and harmony are naturally occurring; they happen without our efforts. They are, in fact, the natural state of the world until we intervene, causing disharmony with our attempts to control and manipulate life. This disharmony is felt in the form of negativity, anger, resentment, guilt or any other painful feeling. Once disharmony is created, we need a word for its opposite, which is why we speak of peace. If there were no war, there would be no peace either; or rather, peace would be so normal and natural that you wouldn't know any different, like fish being unaware they are swimming in water. Everything in the natural world exists in a state of harmony and balance. Ecosystems develop so that nothing can take over, as predators and prey work together in harmony, each maintaining the other at a sustainable level. Of course, this is only clear when looking from the outside, as it isn't something that is planned by the individual organisms within; it is simply the natural expression of their nature. They work together seamlessly without any thought of working together.

It is the same for us. The word 'co-operation' means that we operate together, simultaneously, without any real thought of working together. This type of action is rare for us. As humans, we are too busy chasing our own personal desires to work together in this way. There is no problem with desires, but if we don't take proper care of them, our desires run wild. We can see this in the human race collectively, with people chasing their own desires, and those of their family or their country, with no comprehension of the consequences. There is no harmony in these actions, no balance, just endless unsatisfied desire.

In life, to be harmonious is both a means and an end. Being harmonious means living in accord and peace not only with other people, but with our thoughts and feelings and everything we encounter, from plants and animals to knives and forks. Harmonising with knives and forks may sound strange, but taking care of seemingly small, insignificant things is very important. In fact, our life is made up of these seemingly small things, but we are not usually interested in them. We are interested in big things, grand projects and lofty dreams, but our day-to-day life, our actual life, is not as interesting to us. Taking care of this life each moment with mindfulness, with awareness, is peace and harmony. Paying attention to brushing our teeth instead of listening to your thoughts is peace, and these small, peaceful moments sustain our lives.

One Thing at a Time

The practice of doing one thing at a time is often emphasised in Zen, and this is the essence of mindfulness. Doing one thing at a time may seem obvious, or you might think that everyone is doing that anyway, but let me explain. Normally, when we do something, our attention is focused on our thoughts, with a little left over for the activity, maybe only just enough to get it done. The rest of our attention is absorbed in thoughts about the past and the future, or about nothing in particular. One exception to this is when we are learning something new, which leads us to pay attention to what we are doing.

According to science, pleasure-producing chemicals are released in the brain when we learn something new, leading people to enjoy learning new things. I wonder if some of this enjoyment comes because thoughts take a back seat for a few moments as we pay close attention to the task at hand. There is no need to disregard this attention once we have mastered the task, as continuing to mindfully do something we find easy brings a great sense of peace and contentment. In Zen master Shunryu Suzuki's classic book *Zen Mind, Beginner's*

Mind [2], he emphasises maintaining this beginner's mind in activity, which means paying attention to what we are doing.

Think back to your first driving lesson, or the first time you did some other difficult thing. Many of us will remember sitting in the car trying to remember what to do and how to co-ordinate the movements. For me, I was so scared of running into someone or something that my mind could only concentrate on learning: I was fully engaged in the task and in the moment. Of course, plenty of unhelpful thoughts arose within this, and I wasn't totally present all through the session, with worries about the future taking up some of my attention, but I was much more present than I normally would have been. Consider this example for yourself and think about how much attention you bring to driving, to washing the dishes, to any everyday activity. Most of us drive from A to B with minimal awareness of what we are doing, absorbed mostly in the mind's chatter. Driving mindfully, with attention and awareness, is not only much more enjoyable, I think it is much safer too!

There is a well-known Buddhist teaching that says the key to enlightenment is this: 'When you're hungry, eat. When you're tired, sleep.' This doesn't sound too 'spiritual', but it is the essence of mindfulness, which is to narrow your focus to this moment. This means that when you are hungry, *just eat*, don't do anything other

2   Suzuki, Shunryu, *Zen Mind, Beginner's Mind,* New York and Tokyo: Weatherhill, 1970.

than eating: no planning, no daydreaming, no dwelling on the past, just aware, conscious eating. When it is time to go to sleep, just do that without bringing along something extra like thoughts about tomorrow. Whatever you are doing, just do that, be alert and aware.

The key teaching of mindfulness is to bring so much attention to what we are doing *right now* that we no longer get lost in the mind's stories. We can then enjoy our lives as a story, as a wonderful drama, comedy or whatever, without being thrown this way and that by external events. So when we practise mindfulness, we can bring to it this spirit of 'one thing at a time', continuing to notice what is occurring now as well as noticing the thoughts that arise, without getting lost in them.

Quality

As mindfulness starts to permeate throughout our lives, the quality of our actions changes. The awareness that arises through practising mindfulness makes us more effective, kinder, more peaceful and more organised. When we aren't lost in thoughts, we can focus completely on the task in front of us. We can listen completely to friends, family and work colleagues instead of thinking about what we will say next. We can also put 100% of our energy into living the best life we can instead of trying to control other people and fighting with our thoughts and feelings. This leaves us free to let others be as they are, without needing them to change in order to keep us happy. Without the need to control others, relationships run more smoothly, life is more enjoyable and people are naturally drawn to us. When the alternative is a life of pain and confusion – partly living, partly lost – it is unimaginable that anyone would choose anything but a life of mindfulness once they have tasted it and seen that it is possible. That life can be your life.

In this section, we have looked at mindfulness in action and examined what life is like living in the present moment. Before we move on to some of the common obstacles you may encounter on the path, please join me for a cup of tea.

A Cup of Tea

Drinking a cup of tea is something billions of people do every day, and it is a good example of an everyday aspect of life, in which you can be mindful or not. It is also a great mindfulness exercise, which we will explore later in the chapter, but for now, let's look at two different ways to drink that cup of tea.

Monday Morning

It's Monday morning, and the alarm goes off. You hit snooze twice (for that extra fourteen minutes of sleep) and then drag yourself out of bed at the third attempt.

You jump in the shower, still half-asleep, make yourself presentable and head to the kitchen for breakfast. After chomping your way through a bowl of cereal, you put the kettle on, aware that you have only ten minutes until you have to leave. You take a cup, throw in a teabag, pour the water – spilling some – then dunk the teabag a few times before quickly pouring in the milk. You add some cold water as you now have only five minutes left. You gulp down your tea, half-listening to the radio, half-thinking about what you have to do at work that day, and watching the clock out of the corner of your eye. Time to go, so you put your cup in the sink, hopefully remember to put the milk back in the fridge, and run out of the door.

This is the way we drink our tea, and it is also the way we live our lives: running from one thing to the next, barely aware of what we are doing at the time, thinking about the past, planning for the future, trying to get things done so we can get to a point where we have everything under control and we can finally relax. Ironically, all this adds up to stress, anxiety and a life barely experienced – a life of absence. To step out of this life, which is the life society dictates, is a revolution, and that is what mindfulness is all about. I barely tasted that last cup, so let's share another one...

Sunday Afternoon

It is a lazy Sunday afternoon, and the glow of the sun is streaming through the kitchen window. You look outside and notice a bird feeding in the garden as the trees sway in the breeze. You breathe in and notice the feeling of your lungs expanding, the sound of the air exiting your lungs, the sensation of the air entering your nostrils. As you walk into the kitchen, you feel the tiles under your feet and notice the way your feet connect with the floor. You pick up the kettle and examine it, taking in every detail as you carefully fill it with water. As the kettle begins to boil, you listen to the sound it makes while carefully taking a teacup from the cupboard and placing it on the side. You take out a teabag and place it gently in the cup, then walk slowly over to the fridge. Opening the fridge, you notice the vibrant colours of all the food inside and feel the cool air blowing across your skin. You close the fridge and return to the cup, lifting the kettle and carefully pouring the boiling water over the teabag. You pause for a moment and watch the steam rising from the cup before replacing the kettle. While the tea steeps, you pause and take a long, slow breath. You look out the window once again and notice a second bird feeding in the garden. You remove the teabag, add the milk and put it back in the fridge before walking into the garden and sitting down with your cup of tea. You watch the steam rising as you take a sip, paying attention to the warmth of the liquid, the taste, the colour. You put the cup down and breathe. As you sit in the garden, you savour each instant of the experience, totally focused on this activity, this place. Having finished your cup of tea, you sit for a few minutes more before slowly returning to the kitchen.

A Mindful Cup of Tea

Now, to fully understand the difference between these two cups of tea, it is important to experience a 'mindful' cup of tea, otherwise it will remain a mental concept, just a thought in your head. So, if you are at home, go to the kitchen and make yourself a cup of tea, coffee or whatever you like to drink.

1 Act as if you were the emperor's head servant and do everything with as much care, concentration and precision as you can.

2 Notice what it feels like to walk to the kitchen, what you can hear, see, smell and feel.

3 Treat the drink as if it were your last on Earth and savour every mouthful.

Notice how this differs from your usual cup of tea. It is possible to be mindful every time we drink anything, and it begins now. Every day is made up of events like this, one after another, and we can experience peace and happiness just by being aware, by paying attention to each thing we do. See how mindful you can be today and notice what it is like to bring this awareness to each activity. This is the path of peace.

The exercises we have carried out together can provide your mindfulness practice and your happiness with a strong foundation, but you may still run into some difficulties along the way. The following chapter explores some of the obstacles you may encounter and provides some simple tips for overcoming them. I hope that these suggestions make the path a little easier to navigate, and that you can sidestep some of the challenges I ran into when I first sat down to meditate.

PART THREE
Walking the Path

Practising mindfulness and making it part of our lives is challenging and requires effort. Along the path, obstacles inevitably arise, not because mindfulness is difficult, but because our minds are so complicated. What follows in this chapter is by no means an exhaustive list, but it describes some of the most common challenges experienced by new practitioners and old hands alike.

CHAPTER NINE

Smoothing the Path: Overcoming obstacles in your practice

Expectations

As people, we generally approach any new endeavour with goals and expectations about what we will get from it, and mindfulness is no exception. We all come to mindfulness, or any other meditation practice, for a reason: we want to change something, find peace or attain some other goal. These goals serve an important purpose: they bring us to the beginning of the journey, to a book, a workshop, a retreat. However, once you start to practise, goals and expectations start to get in the way if you don't know how to take proper care of them. For example, many of us start to practise with the goal of being more peaceful or finding happiness, but when we start to meditate, we may find just the opposite. We may first have to sit down with anger, with guilt, with boredom, with the parts of ourselves we don't like. Mindfulness is about being aware of our present moment experience with an attitude of openness and curiosity, so we just observe whatever arises rather than trying to get rid of what we hate and hang on to what we like. A narrow focus on 'peace' or 'happiness' leaves no room to experience the other emotions we face as a part of our daily lives. When expectations arise, just notice them, become aware of them as you would any other thought. See what happens when you acknowledge these thoughts and continually return your attention to the present moment. You may notice the mind creating the story of 'my practice and my progress', talking about how well (or how badly) you are doing. Treat this like any other story; watch it come and go, and keep paying attention to this instant.

Mental Noise

When learning to practise mindfulness, the first thing most people notice is how noisy, busy and uncontrollable the mind is. When I first started to meditate, staying focused on my breath for five seconds seemed pretty amazing, as my mind was so busy and seemed so cunning in luring me away from this moment. This was a source of great frustration for me, and meditation became grave and dreary at times. A few years later, I was listening to a talk from a great Zen teacher about leaving and returning. He was describing what happens when we bring attention to the present moment, but are then drawn away by the mind into some fantasy.

What he said was that meditation is about coming back to this moment, again and again, so we need not be discouraged when the mind draws us away. If you are even just thirty years old, you have probably spent at least twenty-five years or more engrossed in the mind's ceaseless chatter, and expecting to change that habit in a day, a week or a year is just the mind setting unrealistic goals. This is what your mind naturally does, but there is no need to listen to it. Instead, we can go beyond those expectations by becoming aware of them without getting caught up in them. This means just treating these thoughts like any other, noticing them and bringing our attention back to the present moment. This is an ongoing practice that gets stronger over time, but it is challenging in the beginning.

Wavering Commitment

A key point in my classes and workshops is the difficulty of the task we are undertaking when we begin mindfulness practice, and the commitment required to go beyond believing our thoughts. It isn't difficult in the same way that quantum physics is difficult; you don't need a lot of intellectual knowledge to learn mindfulness. What you need is to keep practising, day after day, to keep returning your attention to *now*, moment after moment, to keep noticing that you are lost and returning to this moment. It isn't complicated; in fact, it is too simple to keep the mind entertained, which is what makes it so difficult to practise. We are conditioned to seek stimulation and activity and to associate silence and stillness with boredom or laziness, so sitting and paying attention to your surroundings for twenty minutes may seem like a complete waste of time to the mind. This is why we try to find a reason to practise, like finding peace, or seeking enlightenment, which is much more interesting to the mind as it provides a goal, something to work towards for the future.

Continuing to practise when you don't seem to be 'getting anywhere' requires persistence and patience, and it is common to stop practising for periods of time, returning to mindfulness later on.

The source of the discouragement is often unmet expectations, which can be taken care of by becoming aware of them without chasing them, as discussed earlier.

Seeking in the Future

Closely related to goals and expectations are future projections of what things will be like when you have mastered mindfulness. We saw in Part One that this is a normal thing for the mind to occupy itself with, but it also pulls our attention away from now. What we are doing in mindfulness practice is sitting, aware of this moment, without getting drawn into future goals, including enlightenment. Therefore, we must learn to sit without the expectation of getting something from it, and we can start by noticing these projections and fantasies about the future as they arise, being aware of them, and trying not to chase them or play with them.

Intellectualising

Humans, especially in the West, love to think, to analyse, to spin philosophy – or rather the mind loves to do these things. Mindfulness is something we *do*, not something we *ponder*. It must be experienced or it is totally useless, like talking about food when you are hungry. Reading, discussing and thinking about mindfulness keeps us at a safe distance, like reading travel guides instead of going somewhere in case you get robbed. Books, internet resources and discussion can provide encouragement, practical advice and insight, but if you aren't practising day by day, then this research is no more than preparation. Mindfulness is a practice, not a concept, so be sure that intellectualising is not primary in your practice. Doing must be primary, with reading being like a vitamin supplement you take to strengthen your body and mind, not a replacement food. Be wary of the urge to escape into books instead of experiencing what is.

Preferences

In Zen, they often say when you do sitting meditation, 'just sit', or when you do walking meditation, 'just walk'. Sometimes this is the only instruction students get, and really it is all they need. 'Just sitting' means sitting down with awareness in the middle of everything that is going on around us, whether our mind is peaceful or not, whether we experience joyful feelings or not. This is very hard to do, as we are so used to trying to shape our experiences in accordance with our preferences – our likes and dislikes. When we practise mindfulness, we learn to go beyond these preferences. We treat feelings of anger and feelings of joy in the same way, which is the beginning of the end of struggling with emotions, of avoiding some and chasing others. Without this struggle, we can enjoy all aspects of life and things naturally become more peaceful.

Keeping Score

As we practise at home and in daily life, the mind is often keen to keep score of 'how mindful I am', which is quite funny. If we are thinking about how mindful we are being, we are lost in our heads, unaware that our practice has gone out of the window at that moment. The mind tries to keep track of the level of mindfulness and then projects that into the future to predict what will happen, but this 'future-watching' takes us out of now and makes things unnecessarily complicated. If we can start with just one mindful breath, that is very good. In fact, just one breath is all we can ever do, so be as mindful as possible for this breath, then forget about it and focus on the next breath. If you are walking, be aware of just one step, then leave it behind. If we start thinking, 'Wow, I was really mindful on that last breath. My practice is getting really strong!' we are already lost. This is what the mind does; it compares, analyses and evaluates, but in mindfulness, we can allow this part of the mind to have a rest. Instead, we can learn to observe this process without getting carried away by the mind's judgements. To do this, come back to the awareness of this breath, of this step. There is nothing more to it than that. Every time you realise you are lost in thought, come back to just one breath, just one step. In this breath, there is peace, there is quiet, even if the mind is noisy and agitated. Taking care of this one step, we take care of our whole life, which is made up of millions of moments, of this step, then this step and so on. So, as you go about your daily life, keep coming back to this breath and this step and see what happens. It will surprise you.

Distractions

If you are like most people, doing these exercises will bring your mind's activity into sharper focus. In other words, the constant mental noise in the form of thoughts, images and memories can seem louder when we pay attention to reality. As any honest meditation student will tell you, it is also normal to get distracted by thoughts again and again. The aim of mindfulness is not to block or silence this mental activity, but to become aware of it. Whatever arises during mindfulness practice, whether it is a thought, a feeling, a sound or some other aspect of reality, we simply become aware of it. Thoughts appear mesmerising, and they tend to attract our full attention. When this happens, and you notice that you are lost in thought, all you need to do is to return your attention to reality, or in other words, come back to *now*. A good way to do this is to return your attention to the breath, take a couple of mindful breaths and return your attention to the activity you are engaged in. The five senses are also a valuable tool in mindfulness practice, as the sights, smells, tastes, sounds and sensations that we experience every moment can help us to remain anchored in the present moment.

Overcoming Difficulty

Overcoming difficulty really means learning *to be* with difficulty, to accept it happily and peacefully. This is not something to 'work on', but it happens naturally when we are not lost in our minds, believing the thoughts that come and go. Whatever arises, all that we ever need to do is to bring our attention back to now, regardless of what distracted us. Expectations, projections, worries, comparisons, they are all thoughts, so treat them like any other thought – notice them and return to the moment. This is far more effective than ignoring or trying to get rid of those thoughts, which are a part of our experience at that moment. Instead, we can simply come back, again and again, to now. Any time you get frustrated because you can't relax, your mind is too busy, mindfulness is too hard – whatever the story may be – notice what your mind is telling you at that moment. What thoughts are you believing? Pain and confusion can only come from believing thoughts, which are often confusing and painful. Start to notice these thoughts and notice what happens when you believe them. This is the beginning of peace.

CHAPTER TEN

Questions and Answers

Here are some of the common questions people ask in the workshops I teach.

If you have any further questions, please go to my website at: www.mindfulnessplainandsimple.com and send me a message.

How Much Time Should I Spend Practising Mindfulness?

It really depends on the individual. Find what works within your life and adjust as needed. It is more important to practise regularly than it is to practise for long periods, so ten minutes every day will give your practice more stability than doing two hours in one go on a Sunday night. Practise as often as you can and try to maintain this awareness throughout the day. Finding online resources (videos, podcasts, etc.) is another great way to maintain regular practice. Byron Katie and

Eckhart Tolle are two teachers I highly recommend – check the resources at the end of the book for their websites. My own podcast series is hosted at www. alittlepeaceandquiet.com and provides a brief, simple class every weekday.

How Often Should I Practise?

Again, this is up to you. Once a day is good, once a week is good. The more you practise, the more settled you will become as you get used to mindful sitting and walking. Regular formal practice also makes it easier to do informal practice, so do it as often as is practical. If possible, plan your practice the day before and stick to your plan. For example, if you intend to get up at 6 a.m. and practise for half an hour, try setting up the space and laying out your clothes before you go to bed. Then, when the alarm goes off, get up and meditate, regardless of what your mind tells you. In a sense, this is the beginning of our practice because when the mind says 'You're too tired, just have another half-hour in bed', we can practise noticing this thought without believing it, arguing with it, or getting lost in it.

My Partner/Friend/Mother/Boss Needs to Learn Mindfulness. How Can I Teach Them?

The answer to this is simple and freeing. You cannot teach anyone mindfulness unless they want to learn, but you can show how peaceful and joyful life can be when you are anchored in the present moment. In my experience, this is the best way to teach, by simply being here now.

How Can I Deal with Conflict Mindfully?

As you become more adept at watching thoughts and embracing emotions, conflict in daily life starts to evaporate. When it does arise, the way to handle it is to deal with those thoughts and emotions mindfully; watch thoughts, sit with emotions and don't let the dramatic stories take over. And if you do get lost in drama, when you come back to the present an apology and a smile goes a long way.

What Should I Think about during Meditation?

The point of mindfulness is to learn to observe thoughts instead of getting caught up in them, so try to allow thoughts to come and go without getting lost. When you do get lost, simply notice this and return to this instant.

What if I Can't Remove All the Distractions?

We do our best to remove as many distractions as possible. Any unavoidable distractions become part of our practice. So, for example, if the dog next door barks incessantly during your meditation, notice this sound without judgement. If judgements and comments arise, notice them and return your attention to the moment. In this way, these distractions can even support your practice.

Why Don't I Feel Peaceful?

As mentioned earlier, mindfulness doesn't mean having a quiet mind, it means being aware of the mind without getting lost in it. So, whatever your mind is like right now, just experience it. Your mind may be trying to 'get' peace by practising mindfulness, but this process of trying to get somewhere causes noise, so there can be no peace. If this is the case, you might feel anxious, stressed or annoyed, and your mind may become frustrated at your apparent lack of progress. Just feel that anger, that frustration, be with it without running from it or resisting it, allow yourself to fully experience it. This brings you back to this moment instead of listening to your mind's story about why things should be peaceful.

I Can't Meditate. My Mind Is Too Noisy.

Many people's minds tell them this story, but you can be mindful whether your mind is noisy or not. This is a bit like saying you are too unfit to do exercise. It will be challenging, yes, but if you can maintain your practice over time, your mind will become more settled, more peaceful. Don't worry about the results, just start today and practise without any idea of getting something from it.

I Am Too Busy to Practise Mindfulness.

Is that so? Try to notice what you do instead of setting aside time for formal practice. Can you spot a ten- or fifteen-minute gap where you are just killing time by watching TV or playing on the internet? Would you rather watch the TV for an extra hour or practise something that brings peace and joy into your life? If you would rather practise, then just do it, and stop thinking about why you can't fit it in.

Finally...

Over the course of this book, we have gone on a journey, from exploring the dysfunction of the human mind, to seeing what else is possible, to experiencing mindfulness for ourselves. This, however, is the start of the real journey to wholeness, which is there when we stop seeking happiness and fulfilment outside of ourselves. The patterns of the mind are strongly ingrained and, at times, emotions can become so strong that they completely overwhelm us; this is the reality for most people. If you experience these challenges along the way, worry not! When you realise that you have become lost in a thought or emotion, just bring your attention back to this moment, again and again. Nothing else is needed. Over time, if you continue to meditate, these thoughts and emotions will have less power over you and you will discover freedom. Know that there is nothing else you need for your happiness, nothing to get, nothing to do, and nowhere to go. When you realise this, not as a belief but as an experience, then you can happily go to places, do things and make your way in the world without getting lost in it. This is integrated practice, living mindfully, and it is the natural state of all humans, which is why living through the mind is so painful. Returning to this natural state of peace and freedom is possible for everyone, and it is as simple as practising mindfulness, returning your attention to now each time you get lost in a thought. Deepen this practice of paying attention to now, and you will be richly rewarded. Peace and happiness will be your companions and problems will slowly disappear. May your path be smooth, may the road be peaceful, and may you attain freedom from the mind. Thank you.

And if you haven't been there already, remember to visit www.mindfulnessplainandsimple.com to download the free audio series that accompanies this book.

Resources

Byron Katie – www.thework.com
Eckhart Tolle – www.eckharttolle.com
Thich Nhat Hanh – www.plumvillage.org
Zen in Australia – www.jikishoan.org.au
Adyashanti – www.adyashanti.org
Smiling Mind – www.smilingmind.com.au
Everyday Mindfulness – www.everyday-mindfulness.org

For competitions, author interviews,
pre-publication extracts, news and events,
sign up to the monthly

Orion Books Newsletter

at

www.orionbooks.co.uk

Prefer your updates daily?
Follow us @orionbooks